CAMBRIDGE PRIMARY MATHEMATICS

BOOK 2

Roy Edwards
Mary Edwards
Alan Ward

Cambridge University Press
Cambridge
New York   Port Chester
Melbourne Sydney

Published by the Press Syndicate of the University of Cambridge
The Pitt Building, Trumpington Street, Cambridge CB2 1RP
40 West 20th Street, New York, NY 10011-4211, USA
10 Stamford Road, Oakleigh, Melbourne 3166, Australia

First published 1991

Printed in Great Britain at the University Press, Cambridge

A catalogue record for this book is available from the British Library.

ISBN 0 521 36723 9

The authors and publisher would like to thank the many schools
and individuals who have commented on draft material for this
course. In particular, they would like to thank Anita Straker for
her contribution to the suggestions for work with computers,
Norma Anderson, Ronalyn Hargreaves (Hyndburn Ethnic
Minority Support Service) and John Hyland (Advisory Teacher
in Tameside).

Photographs are reproduced courtesy of:
front cover ZEFA; p 5 NHPA/Stephen Dalton; p 7 NHPA/Henry Ansloos; p 9 Ronald Sheridan/Ancient Art &
Architecture Collection; Mozart Museum, Salzburg; National Portrait Gallery, London; p 12 Aviemore
Photographic; p 13 Judith Taylor; pp 26, 58, 88, 92 NASA; p 41 ZEFA; p 43 Heather Angel; p 44 ALLSPORT;
p 45 Peter Newark's Western Americana; pp 46, 47, 50 The Hutchison Library; p 81 Fishbourne Roman
Palace/Sussex Archaeological Society; p 102 Ulla Taylor.

All other photographs by Graham Portlock.
The mathematical apparatus was kindly supplied by E J Arnold.

Designed by Chris McLeod

Illustrations by Gordon Hendry and Gary Rees
Diagrams by Oxprint
Children's illustrations by Robert Gilfillan and Louise Sterno

Contents

Number 2

A

Ronika   Age 7

How many months old were these children on their last birthdays?

1 Ronika   2 Marie   3 Sammy

4 Approximately how many days old were they?
Count a year as 365 days.

Ella   Age 5

5 Sammy and Ella have the same birthday.
How many days older is Sammy?

> Every 4th year is a leap year. The number of the year divides exactly by 4.

Marie   Age 9

6 How many days are in a leap year?

7 Copy and complete the chart as far as this year.
Show the leap years.

1984	1985	1986	☐

Leap Year

8 How many days altogether in 1984, 1985 and 1986?

Sammy   Age 8

9 How many leap years have you lived in?
Which were they?

The average lifespan of a gerbil is 104 weeks.

Sammy's gerbil lived for 98 weeks 2 days.

Marie's gerbil lived for 112 weeks.

10 The average life span of a gerbil is ☐ days.

11 How many days did Sammy's gerbil live?

12 How many days did Marie's gerbil live?

13 How many days longer did Marie's gerbil live?

14 Which gerbil lived longer than average?

15 Change these incubation times into weeks and days.
Copy and complete the chart.

Average incubation times		
Bird	Days	Weeks and days
Swan	30	
Thrush	14	
Hawk	44	
Emperor penguin	63	

16 These animals give birth to live young.
What is the average number of weeks and days they are pregnant?
Copy and complete the chart.

Average length of pregnancy		
Mammal	Days	Weeks and days
Goat	151	
Giraffe	410	
Rhinoceros	560	

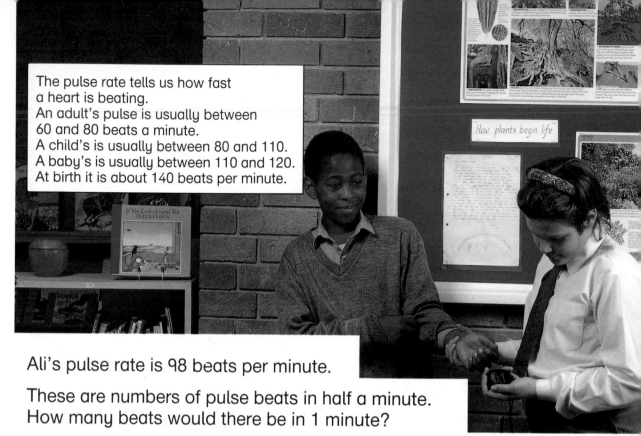

The pulse rate tells us how fast
a heart is beating.
An adult's pulse is usually between
60 and 80 beats a minute.
A child's is usually between 80 and 110.
A baby's is usually between 110 and 120.
At birth it is about 140 beats per minute.

Ali's pulse rate is 98 beats per minute.

These are numbers of pulse beats in half a minute.
How many beats would there be in 1 minute?

17 57 beats   **18** 38 beats   **19** 49 beats   **20** 35 beats

21 Which one is Ali's?

How many beats does Ali's heart make in these times?

22 3 minutes   **23** 5 minutes   **24** 8 minutes

Jolene's pulse rate is 102 beats per minute.
How many times does her heart beat in these times?

25 2 minutes   **26** 5 minutes   **27** 7 minutes

28 What is the difference between Jolene's and Ali's
pulse beats in 5 minutes?

Let's investigate

Find out whether walking, jumping and running change your pulse rate.
Explain how you found out.
Record your findings.

Length of life		
Time	Hours	Minutes
Born 1:30 p.m.	0	0
2:30 p.m.	1	60
3:30 p.m.	2	12

Jolene's dog gave birth to a puppy.
She kept a chart to show how many minutes it had been alive.

1 Make a chart to show the number of minutes
in 2 hours, 4 hours, 6 hours, 8 hours, 10 hours, 12 hours.

2 Explain how you worked out the number of minutes.

Find ways to work these out out in your head.

3 8 × 30

4 11 × 40

5 9 × 50

6 6 × 200

7 4 × 400

8 5 × 200

9 20 × 100

10 30 × 200

11 20 × 400

12 Discuss with a friend how you did them.

Find a way to work these out.

13 32 × 26

14 45 × 13

15 89 × 27

16
```
  133
×  45
─────
```

17
```
  242
×  17
─────
```

18
```
  464
×  36
─────
```

How many hours had Jolene's puppy been alive when it was these ages?

19 14 days old

20 21 days old

21 4 weeks old

22 6 weeks old

23 9 weeks old

24 10 weeks old

25 Approximately how many weeks
do these animals live?

Count a year
as 52 weeks.

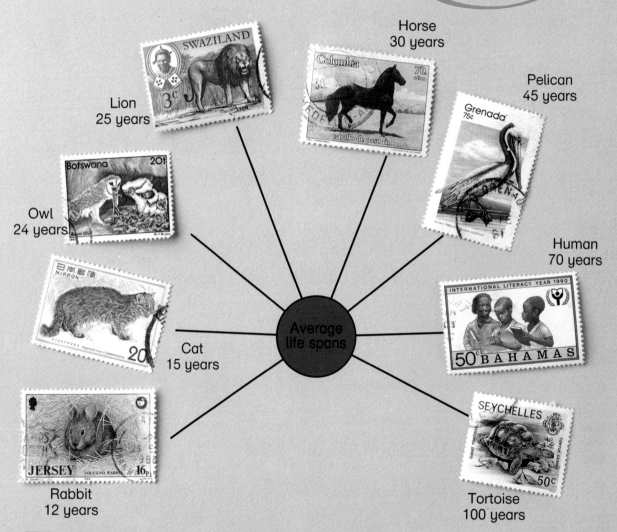

Horse
30 years

Pelican
45 years

Lion
25 years

Owl
24 years

Human
70 years

Cat
15 years

Average
life spans

Rabbit
12 years

Tortoise
100 years

26 Who is the oldest person you know?
Approximately how many weeks had they been
alive on their last birthday?

Approximately how many weeks and days did
these people live?

27 A Japanese man lived
for 120 years 237 days.
He died in 1986.

28 A British woman lived
for 114 years 208 days.
She died in 1987.

Approximately how many days had these famous people been alive on their last birthdays.

Count a year as 365 days

29 Tutankhamen of Egypt

Died at the age of 18

30 Mozart

Died at the age of 35

31 Grace Darling

Died at the age of 26

32 Use your calculator to work out approximately how many minutes you had been alive on your last birthday.

33 What difference would it make if you allowed for leap years?

Let's investigate

Start with these five digits. 5, 3, 9, 2, 7
Use them to make a 3 digit number and a
2 digit number, using each digit once only.
For example, 297 and 35.
Multiply the two numbers.
What is the largest answer you can make
in this way?

C

Most mammals that live to old age have each had approximately 800 000 000 heart beats in their life times. Humans are different. Our natural lifespan has many more heartbeats than the other mammals.

1 An elephant's heart beats about 30 times a minute. A shrew's heart beats almost 1000 times a minute.

Approximately how many times do each of their hearts beat in 1 day?

2 Approximately how many times, to the nearest million, does the shrew's heart beat in a week?

3 Find a way to calculate how many times it will beat in $1\frac{1}{2}$ years? Count a year as 52 weeks. What do you notice about this number and the information at the top of the page?

4 Find a way to work out approximately how long an elephant will have lived when it has had 800 000 000 heart beats.

Let's investigate

Complete the following and explain the pattern.

$143 \times 14 =$
$143 \times 21 =$
$143 \times 28 =$
$143 \times 35 =$
$143 \times 42 =$

Number 3

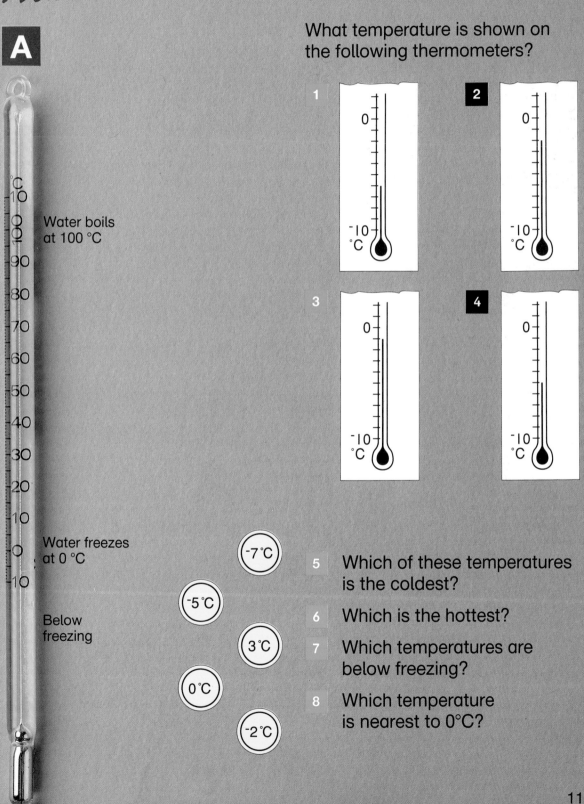

Water boils
at 100 °C

Water freezes
at 0 °C

Below
freezing

What temperature is shown on the following thermometers?

1

2

3

4

-7°C

-5°C

3°C

0°C

-2°C

5 Which of these temperatures is the coldest?

6 Which is the hottest?

7 Which temperatures are below freezing?

8 Which temperature is nearest to 0°C?

11

The graph below shows the temperatures for 24 hours in Aviemore, Scotland.

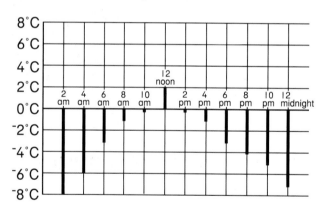

9 What was the temperature at midnight?

10 At what times was it zero?

11 What was the temperature at 6 p.m?

12 What was the hottest temperature?

13 What was the coldest temperature?

14 Write other things about the temperature graph.

This table shows the temperatures for a winter day in Buxton, Derbyshire.

Time	2 a.m.	4 a.m.	6 a.m.	8 a.m.	10 a.m.	12 noon	2 p.m.	4 p.m.	6 p.m.	8 p.m.	10 p.m.	12 midnight
°C	⁻6	⁻4	⁻4	⁻2	⁻1	0	1	0	⁻1	⁻3	⁻5	⁻5

15 Copy the grid and show the temperatures on it.

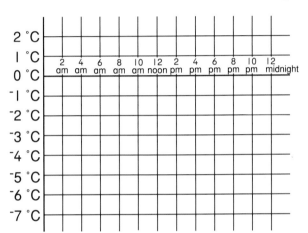

16 At what times was the temperature at freezing point?

17 How many degrees below zero was the coldest temperature?

18 When was the hottest temperature?

19 How many degrees below zero was it at midnight?

Let's investigate

Make up different symbols for the television weather forecast map.
Explain what each symbol means.
Write a temperature to match each symbol.
Some of them must be below zero.

This shows the highest and lowest temperatures one Monday in Bristol.

The range is the difference between highest and lowest.

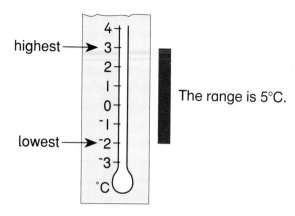

The range is 5°C.

Find the range in temperature for these days.

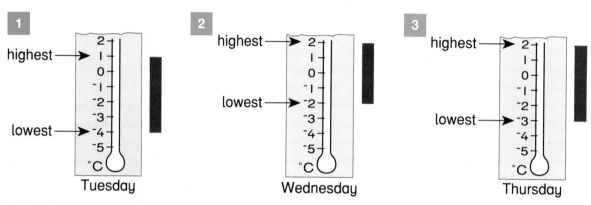

1 Tuesday

2 Wednesday

3 Thursday

4 Friday 1°C and ⁻3°C

5 Saturday 4°C and ⁻1°C

6 Sunday 0°C and ⁻2°C

This table shows the highest and lowest January temperatures in seven cities.

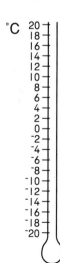

	Highest	Lowest
Belfast	13°C	⁻13°C
Birmingham	13°C	⁻12°C
Cardiff	15°C	⁻17°C
Edinburgh	14°C	⁻8°C
London	14°C	⁻10°C
Plymouth	14°C	⁻9°C
York	15°C	⁻14°C

Find the temperature range for these cities.

7 Birmingham

8 York   **9** Belfast

10 London

11 Edinburgh

12 Plymouth

13 Which city in the table had the greatest range in temperature?

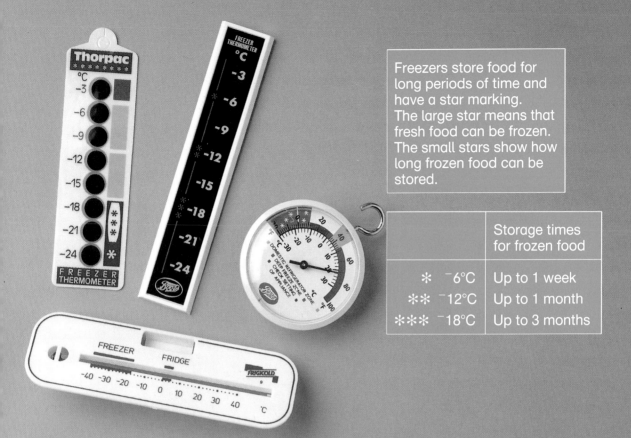

Freezers store food for long periods of time and have a star marking.
The large star means that fresh food can be frozen.
The small stars show how long frozen food can be stored.

		Storage times for frozen food
*	⁻6°C	Up to 1 week
**	⁻12°C	Up to 1 month
***	⁻18°C	Up to 3 months

Find the difference between these storage temperatures.

14 ** and *   **15** *** and **   **16** *** and *

At what temperature should food be stored if it is
to be eaten after these times.

17 3 weeks   **18** 5 days   **19** 10 weeks

If frozen food defrosts to 20°C, how many degrees
have the following temperatures risen?

20 ⁻6°C   **21** ⁻12°C   **22** ⁻18°C

Let's investigate

Show how to get a negative answer on a calculator.
Find as many ways as possible of getting ⁻6.
For example ⁻2−4 = ⁻6

C

This chart shows the temperatures at which different animals can live comfortably.

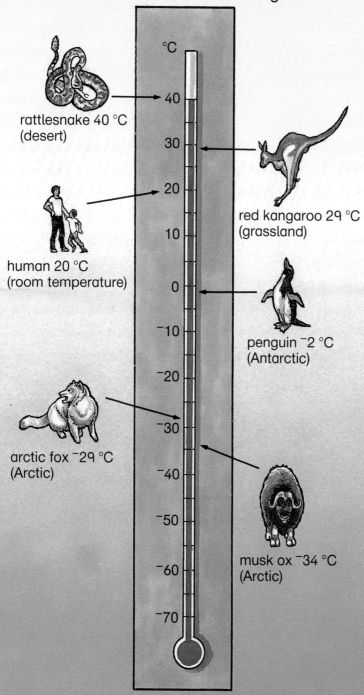

rattlesnake 40 °C (desert)

human 20 °C (room temperature)

red kangaroo 29 °C (grassland)

penguin ⁻2 °C (Antarctic)

arctic fox ⁻29 °C (Arctic)

musk ox ⁻34 °C (Arctic)

Find the difference in temperature between the places where the following animals live.

1 human and penguin

2 human and arctic fox

3 human and musk ox

4 rattlesnake and penguin

5 rattlesnake and arctic fox

6 rattlesnake and musk ox

7 red kangaroo and penguin

8 red kangaroo and arctic fox

9 red kangaroo and musk ox

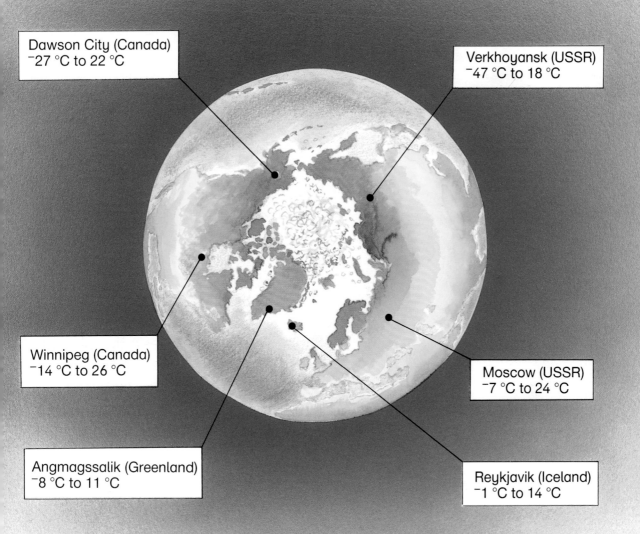

Dawson City (Canada)
⁻27 °C to 22 °C

Verkhoyansk (USSR)
⁻47 °C to 18 °C

Winnipeg (Canada)
⁻14 °C to 26 °C

Moscow (USSR)
⁻7 °C to 24 °C

Angmagssalik (Greenland)
⁻8 °C to 11 °C

Reykjavik (Iceland)
⁻1 °C to 14 °C

These are the temperature ranges of some cities.

10 What is the range in temperature at Moscow?

11 Which place in Canada has the greatest temperature difference? What is it?

12 Which city on the map has the greatest temperature difference? What is it?

13 Design a graph to show the temperature ranges.

Let's investigate

Investigate the factors that influence
the temperature range in different places.

17

The children drew a block graph of their favourite TV programmes.

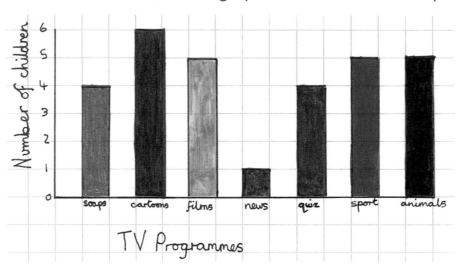

1. Which was the most popular TV programme?

2. Which was the least popular?

3. How many children liked sport?

4. How many children liked quiz programmes?

5. How many children took part in the survey?

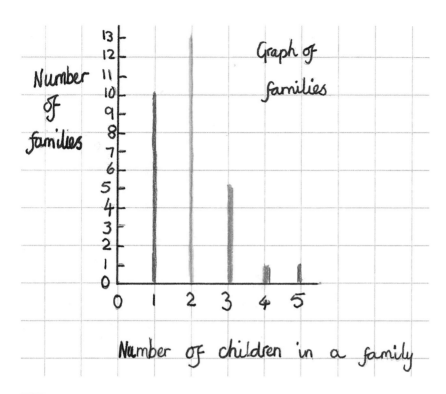

Graph of families

Number of families

Number of children in a family

6 Copy and finish the table using the bar-line graph.

Number of children in a family	1	2	3	4	5
Number of families	10				

7 How many families are there altogether?

8 There are 60 children altogether. What is the mean or average number of children in a family?

This chart shows the number of tickets sold for a school outing.

Tuesday	🔲🔲🔲🔲🔲 ▪
Wednesday	🔲🔲🔲🔲
Thursday	🔲🔲🔲🔲🔲🔲🔲▪
Friday	🔲🔲🔲🔲🔲🔲🔲

🔲 represents 4 tickets

9 Find the total tickets sold on each day.

10 How many more tickets were sold on Friday than on Tuesday?

11 Which day were twice as many tickets sold as on Wednesday?

The children collected data about their interests.

Interest	Tally or frequency
dancing	JHT III
swimming	JHT JHT
cub scouts	II
brownie guides	III
football	JHT II

12 Find the total for each activity.

13 Draw a bar chart for the data. Give it a title and labels.

14 Write some questions about the graph for a friend.

Three of the children collected the ages of everyone in their families.

35	55	6	9	16	5	41	2	72	5
64	32	58	42	59	27	1	46	10	29
23	39	43	18	21	28	60	8	27	52

15 Copy the table and make a tally of the ages.

Ages	Frequency	Totals
0–9		
10–19		
20–29		
30–39		
40–49		
50–59		
60–69		
70–79		

16 Draw a frequency chart to show the data.

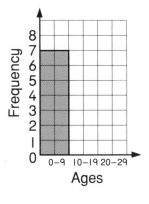

Ages	0–☐	☐–☐	☐–☐	☐–☐
Totals				

17 Group the ages into 4 equal age groups and find the totals.

Explain what is wrong with these groupings of the ages.

18
0–9
10–19
20–29
30–39
40–49

19
0–9
10–39
40–79

20
0–20
20–40
40–60
60–80

This is how John spent a day.

in bed
9 p.m. to 8 a.m.

eating
breakfast 15 mins
dinner 20 mins
tea 20 mins
supper 5 mins

playing
afternoon 1 hour
evening 3 hours

at school
morning $3\frac{1}{4}$ hours
afternoon $2\frac{3}{4}$ hours

watching TV
afternoon 30 mins
evening 90 mins

21 Copy and complete the table for John's day.

Activity	Hours spent
in bed	
eating	
at school	
playing	
watching TV	

22 Draw a bar chart to show the data in your table.

23 Write 2 sentences about the bar chart.

24 What is the total time John spent on the 5 activities?

25 Which 2 activities did John spend exactly half the day doing?

Let's investigate

Choose a day of the week. Write the length of time, to the nearest hour, you spend doing different activities. Draw a graph of your day. Write some questions about your graph for a friend to answer.

B This is a pie chart. It shows the number of boys and girls in a class.

Each part of the circle represents 1 child

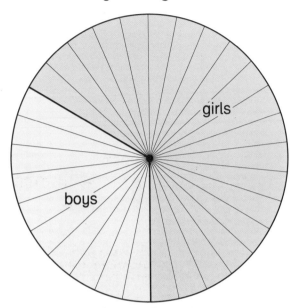

1 How many children are there altogether?

2 How many are boys?

3 How many are girls?

4 What fraction of the children are boys? $\frac{\square}{3}$

5 What fraction are girls? $\frac{\square}{3}$

How long did Ann spend on the following activities?

6 sleeping

7 eating

8 doing homework

9 shopping

10 visiting friends

11 watching TV

What fraction of the day did Ann spend doing the following?

12 shopping **13** eating

How Ann spent a day

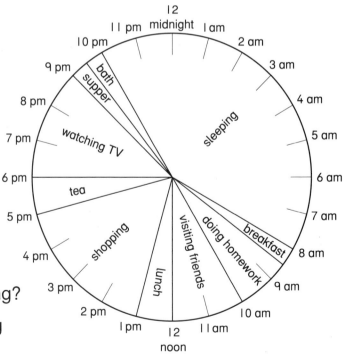

14 Show these 12 hours of a baby's life as a pie chart.

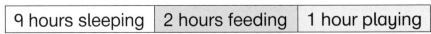

| 9 hours sleeping | 2 hours feeding | 1 hour playing |

22

The chart below shows the height of the children in centimetres.

129	145	135	146	128
151	140	136	141	142
125	134	147	150	144
131	152	133	136	146
141	147	137	148	153
145	128	149	150	147

15 Copy the table below.
Tally the heights of the children from the height chart and write the totals.

Height (cm)	Frequency	Total
121–125		
126–130		
131–135		
136–140		
141–145		
146–150		
151–155		

16 Draw a frequency chart to show the children's heights.

17 Which is the most frequent height?

How many children are between the following heights?

18 121 cm and 130 cm

19 131 cm and 140 cm

20 141 cm and 155 cm

21 121 cm and 155 cm

Let's investigate

Investigate whether, on average, boys or girls of the same age are taller. Explain your findings.

C Ann collected some data from a group of children.

Height (cm)	124	126	146	154	138	158	148	130
Weight (kg)	34	33	37	38	37	41	36	34
Stride Length (cm)	42	44	52	57	46	57	48	47
Height (cm)	144	134	152	150	158	156	124	136
Weight (kg)	38	35	39	39	40	38	33	36
Stride Length (cm)	50	45	56	55	56	52	43	48

She started to draw a scatter graph
showing their heights and weights.

1 Copy and complete the scatter graph using the data above.

Each × represents one child.

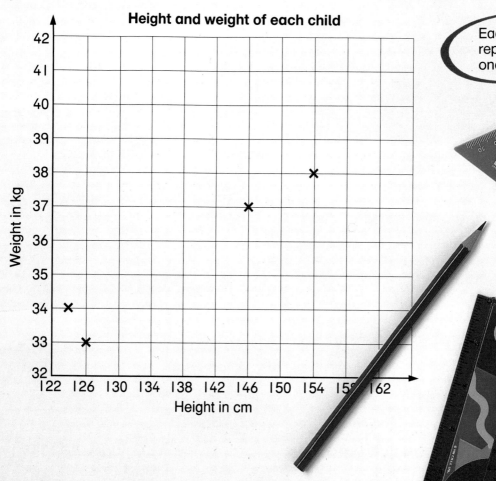

24

2 How many children are represented on your scatter graph?

Use your graph to find how many children are between
the following heights.

3 122 cm and 134 cm   **4** 135 cm and 146 cm

5 147 cm and 162 cm

How many children are between the following weights?

6 32 kg and 34 kg   **7** 35 kg and 37 kg   **8** 38 kg and 42 kg

9 Use Ann's data to complete the following scatter graph
for height and stride length.

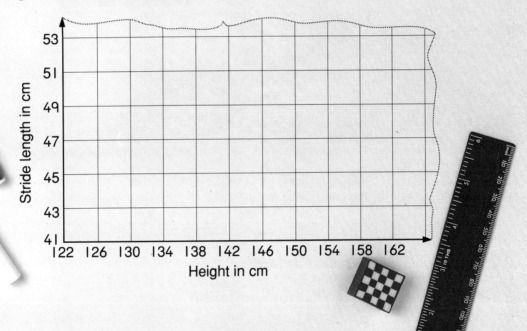

10 Write two sentences about this scatter graph.

11 What does the graph show about the taller children?

Let's investigate

Collect some information about a group of children
that can be shown as a scatter graph.
Draw the graph and explain what it shows.

height
stride
reach
weight

Probability 2

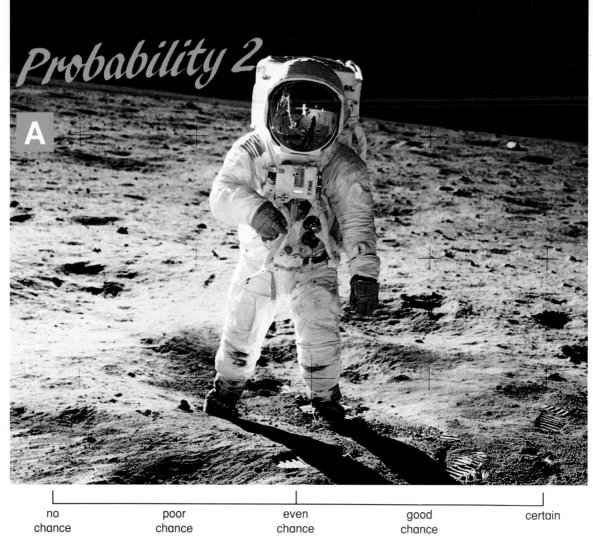

no chance	poor chance	even chance	good chance	certain

Choose the best answer from above for each of these sentences.

1. You will go to the moon next year.

2. You will pilot an aeroplane one day.

3. You will have a bath this week.

4. You will live to be 100 years old.

5. You will play in a pop group one day.

6. You will travel round the world sometime.

7. You will wake up in a good mood tomorrow.

8. You will blink your eyes in the next 5 minutes.

9. You will get a head when you toss a coin.

Blue or Yellow

Put 2 yellow cubes and
1 blue cube in a bag.

Without looking pick one
cube from the bag.
Tally the colour.
Put the cube back in the bag.

Do this 30 times.

	Tally	Total
blue		
yellow		

The winning colour is the one with the
higher total.

10 Play 'Blue or Yellow' by yourself or with a friend.

11 Which has more chance of winning, blue or yellow? Why?

12 Explain how you could make this into a fair game.

13 Use the 3 cubes again.
Draw all the different ways
of arranging the cubes in a line.

28

First Home

Use a different coloured
counter for each player.
Put one on each starting circle.

Use a third counter with X on
one side and O on the other.
Toss this counter.
The player whose sign comes up,
moves forward one place.

The winner is the first
to reach home.

14 Play 'First Home' by
yourself or with a friend.
Which won, O or X?

15 Explain which you think
will win in another game.

16 Play the game again.
Which won, O or X?

17 Have O or X an
equal chance of winning?
Explain your answer.

Let's investigate

Use two dice and two
counters.
Make up a fair game.
Design your own board.
Explain your game.

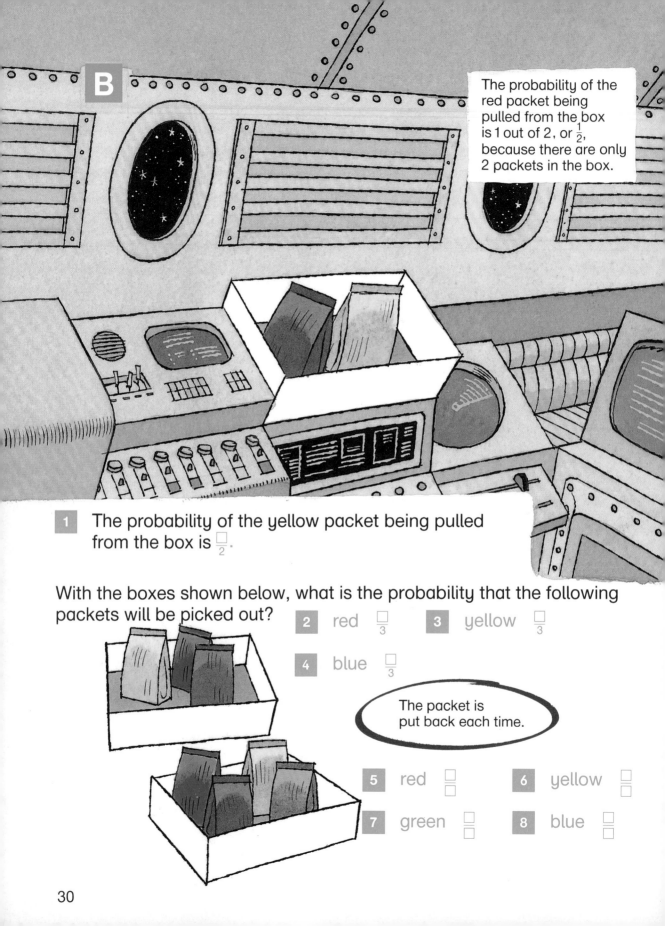

B

The probability of the red packet being pulled from the box is 1 out of 2, or $\frac{1}{2}$, because there are only 2 packets in the box.

1 The probability of the yellow packet being pulled from the box is $\frac{\square}{2}$.

With the boxes shown below, what is the probability that the following packets will be picked out?

2 red $\frac{\square}{3}$ **3** yellow $\frac{\square}{3}$

4 blue $\frac{\square}{3}$

The packet is put back each time.

5 red $\frac{\square}{\square}$ **6** yellow $\frac{\square}{\square}$

7 green $\frac{\square}{\square}$ **8** blue $\frac{\square}{\square}$

Put 1 red reel and 1 blue reel in a pot.
Close your eyes and
pull one out.
Look at it.
Make a tally and
put the reel back.

Do this 20 times.

	Tally	Total
red		
blue		

9 How many of each colour did you pull out?

The following tally charts show the number of times a
coloured reel is pulled out of the pots and replaced.
Use the totals to predict the number of reels of each colour.
Explain your answer each time.

10 2 reels
☐ red
☐ blue

	Tally	Total
red	JHT JHT	10
blue	JHT JHT	10

11 3 reels
☐ red
☐ blue

	Tally	Total
red	JHT JHT JHT JHT	20
blue	JHT JHT	10

12 3 reels
☐ red
☐ blue
☐ yellow

	Tally	Total
red	JHT JHT I	11
blue	JHT IIII	9
yellow	JHT JHT	10

13 4 reels
☐ red
☐ blue

	Tally	Total
red	JHT JHT JHT JHT JHT JHT I	31
blue	JHT IIII	9

What is the probability of these packets being pulled from the boxes?

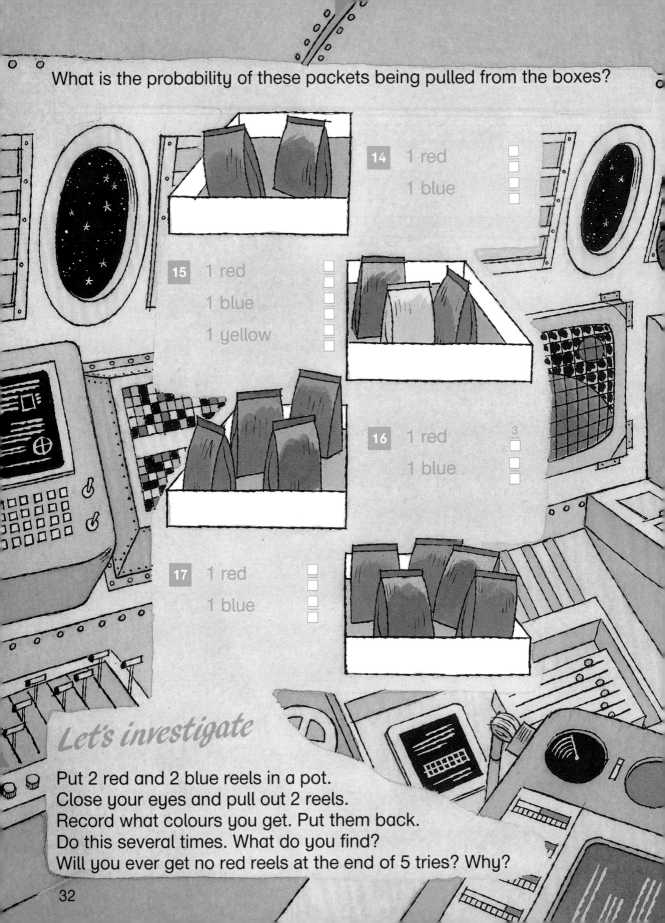

14 1 red

1 blue

15 1 red

1 blue

1 yellow

16 1 red

1 blue

3

17 1 red

1 blue

Let's investigate

Put 2 red and 2 blue reels in a pot.
Close your eyes and pull out 2 reels.
Record what colours you get. Put them back.
Do this several times. What do you find?
Will you ever get no red reels at the end of 5 tries? Why?

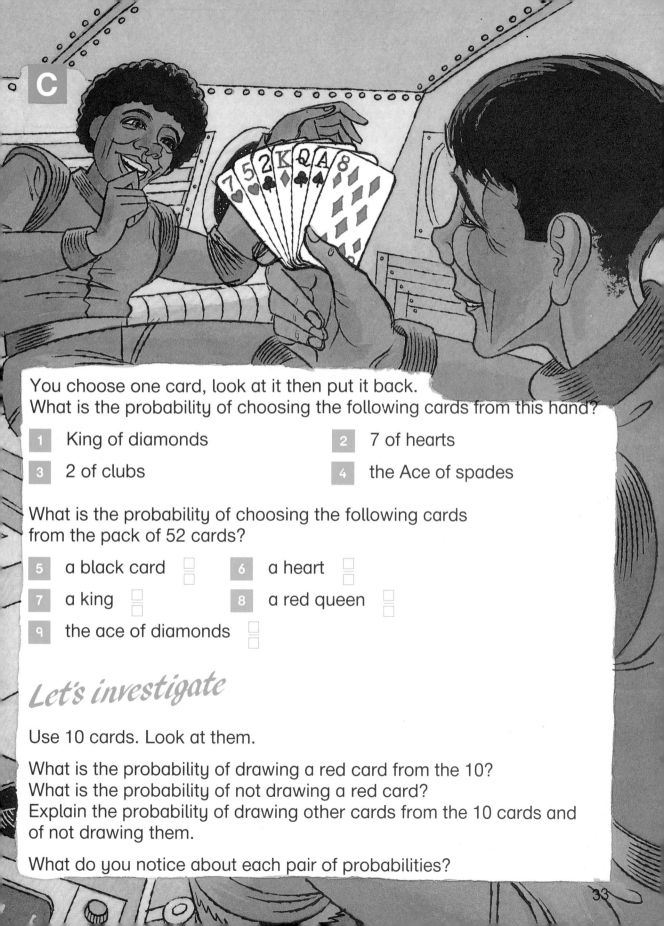

You choose one card, look at it then put it back.
What is the probability of choosing the following cards from this hand?

1 King of diamonds

2 7 of hearts

3 2 of clubs

4 the Ace of spades

What is the probability of choosing the following cards
from the pack of 52 cards?

5 a black card

6 a heart

7 a king

8 a red queen

9 the ace of diamonds

Let's investigate

Use 10 cards. Look at them.

What is the probability of drawing a red card from the 10?
What is the probability of not drawing a red card?
Explain the probability of drawing other cards from the 10 cards and
of not drawing them.

What do you notice about each pair of probabilities?

Angles 1

A

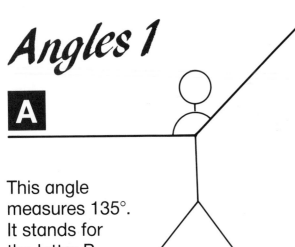

This angle measures 135°. It stands for the letter P.

In a story called 'The Adventure of the Dancing Men' the famous detective Sherlock Holmes has to work out some secret messages which are drawn with stick men like these.

This story was written by Sir Arthur Conan Doyle.

The stick people on these pages are making letters which spell a name.

1 Measure each angle. Look at the code to see which letter it represents.

You need a protractor or angle measurer.

Code	
A	10°
B	20°
C	25°
D	35°
E	45°
F	50°
G	60°
H	65°
I	70°
J	80°
K	90°
L	100°
M	110°
N	120°
O	130°
P	135°
Q	140°
R	150°
S	160°
T	170°
U	180°
V	190°
W	200°
X	210°
Y	220°
Z	230°

2 What is the word?

3 Measure these angles and write their letters.

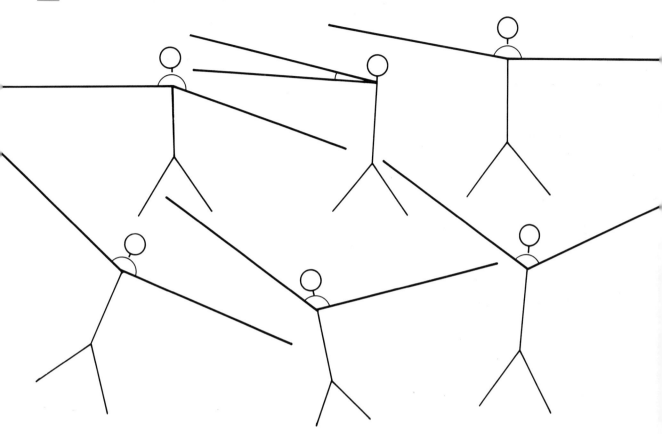

4 What name do the letters make? Who was he?

5 Which of the letters in the word is a reflex angle? Draw the angle.

6 Which of the letters are obtuse angles?

7 Sherlock Holmes lived in Baker Street.
Draw an angle for each letter in Baker.

A reflex angle is between 180° and 360°.

Let's investigate

Is it possible to draw a quadrilateral with a reflex angle and 3 acute angles?
Is it possible to draw a quadrilateral with 4 acute angles?
If you can, draw them.
Investigate drawing quadrilaterals with other sets of angles.

B

> If shapes have the same shape and size they are congruent.

1 Find which of these shapes are congruent.

2 Which is the odd one out?

3 Use templates to draw pairs of congruent quadrilaterals for a friend to match.

4   Trace the silhouette (A) of Holmes' hat.

5   Use the tracing to find which of the other silhouettes are congruent with it. You can turn your tracing over to see if it fits.

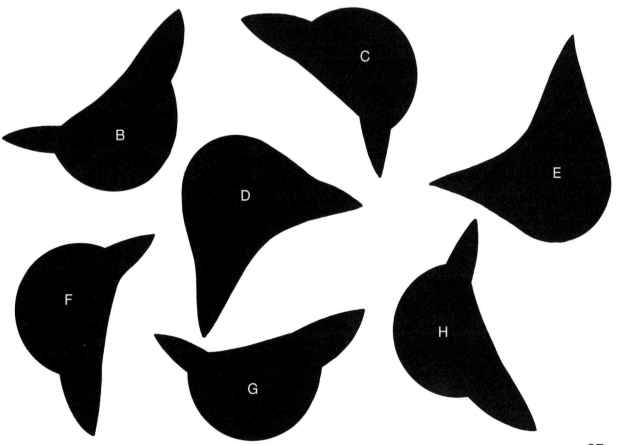

6 Draw a reflex angle of 210°.

7 How big is angle X?

8 What do you notice about the sum
of the two angles?
Can you explain this?

9 Measure another reflex angle. Predict what
angle X will be this time. Check your prediction.

10 Is it possible to draw a triangle with a reflex angle?
Explain your answer.

Investigate the
angles.

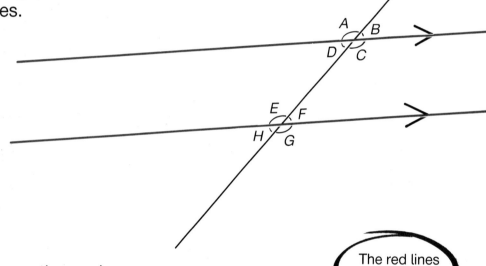

11 Measure the angles.
Which ones are equal in size?

The red lines
are parallel.

12 What do you notice about different pairs of angles?
Explain your findings.

Let's investigate

Use just 4 lines.
Try to make as many angles as you
can that are the same size.

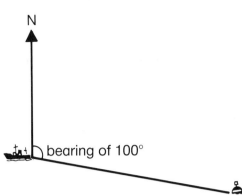

bearing of 100°

Bearings are used to show people like pilots and ships' navigators the direction in which to travel. Bearings are measured from north. It is easy to find north with a compass.

The bearing of the buoy from the ship is the clockwise angle between the north line at the ship and the line from the ship to the buoy.

A bearing always has 3 digits.

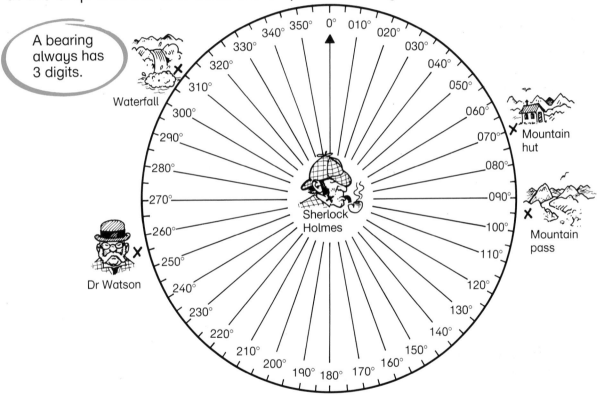

Find the bearing of each of these from Sherlock Holmes.

1 Mountain hut   **2** Waterfall   **3** Mountain pass   **4** Dr Watson

Use a circular protractor. Measure and draw the bearing from Sherlock Holmes to each of these.

5 Alpine village 160°   **6** Hotel 225°

7 Mountain 055°   **8** Lake 270°

9 Sherlock Holmes solved the mystery in 'The Hound of the Baskervilles'. Write the bearings from Baskerville Hall to each of the places on this imaginary plan.

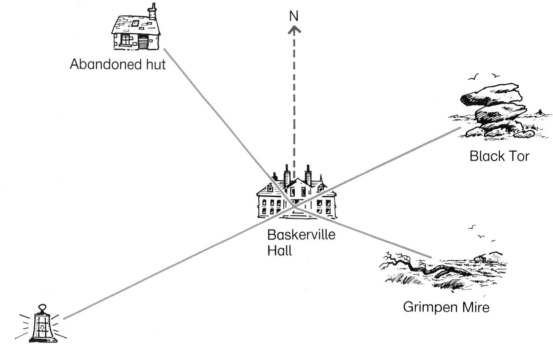

N

Abandoned hut

Black Tor

Baskerville Hall

Grimpen Mire

Concealed signal light

10 If the scale is 1 cm : 1 km how far is it from Baskerville Hall to the abandoned hut, as the crow flies?

11 Choose a place from a mystery or adventure story. Plan the distances and bearings from it to 4 other places mentioned in the story.
Use a 1 cm : 1 km scale.
Ask a friend to draw the plan from your measurements.

Let's investigate

Mark a pair of places on a plan.
Measure the bearing from the first place to the second, then from the second place to the first one.
Do the same with other pairs of places.
What do you notice about each pair of bearings? Can you explain this?

Measurement 1

A

The USA is about thirty-seven times the area of the United Kingdom. The Capital city is Washington.

Some of the earliest Europeans to settle in America were Quakers. They introduced the craft of patchwork.

The patchworks below have been drawn using a scale of 1 cm : 5 cm.

Measure and copy them.

Find their real measurements.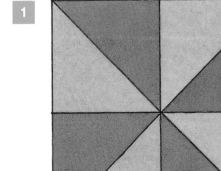
Write them on your drawings.

1 cm : 5 cm means that 1 cm represents 5 cm.

1

2

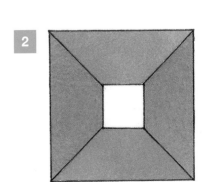

Look at the measurements of this large sign board.

20 m

8 m

Draw the outline of the sign board to these different scales.
Draw them on top of one another starting with
the same bottom left corner each time.

3 1 cm : 1 m   **4** 1 cm : 2 m   **5** 1 cm : 4 m

6 What do you notice about the sides of
your scale drawing each time?

7 What do you notice about the area of
your scale drawing each time?

8 What do you think will happen to the
scale drawing if you use the scale 1 cm : 8 m?

9 Draw it to check your answer.

The sequoia trees in California are conifers and are very tall. The Howard Libbey redwood is 110 m tall and is the world's tallest tree.

The Howard Libbey redwood is 110 m high.
An English oak can grow to 30 m high.

Draw lines to show the heights of the two trees.

10 Use a 1 cm : 5 m scale.

11 Use a of 1 cm : 10 m scale.

12 What do you notice about your scale drawings?

13 How high would the lines be if the scale was 1 cm : 2 m?

14 Cut strips of paper to show the three scales for the trees. Stick them in your book.

Baseball is a very popular sport in America. To score a run, a player must run round the baseball diamond after hitting the ball.

15 This is a plan of a baseball pitch.
Draw it on a 1 cm : 2 m scale.
Use paper if it will not fit in your book.

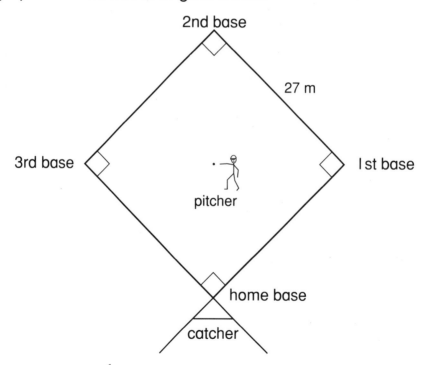

2nd base

27 m

3rd base

pitcher

1st base

home base

catcher

Let's investigate

Find out the measurements of a sports pitch or court for a game you have played or watched.
Work out a scale that you could use to draw it in your book.

B

The first Americans were the Indians. Later, Europeans settled and as they moved west across America they built pioneer villages.

Part of a Pioneer Village is shown below.
It is drawn to a scale of 1 : 100.

1. If the plan shows a length of 1 cm, what length is the real object?

2. Write the real measurements of the three buildings.

log cabin

general store

blacksmith's shop

America has some of the world's tallest buildings.

Empire State Building, New York   381 m
Sears Building, Chicago   443 m
World Trade Centre, New York   412 m
Chrysler Building, New York   318 m

3   What does 1 cm represent in cm on a 1 : 100 scale?

4   What does 1 cm represent in m on a 1 : 100 scale?

5   How tall would you draw each of the four buildings above on a 1 : 100 scale?
Complete the table.

Actual height	Height on 1 : 100 scale		
381 m	☐ cm	☐ m	☐ cm
443 m	☐ cm	☐ m	☐ cm
412 m	☐ cm	☐ m	☐ cm
318 m	☐ cm	☐ m	☐ cm

6   The tallest office block in England is 183 m tall.
How tall would you make it on a 1 : 100 scale?
How tall on a 1 : 50 scale? What do you notice?

7   Measure your classroom and draw it on a 1 : 50 scale.

On the flag of the USA each star represents a state.

Look at this drawing of the Texas state flag.

8   Draw the flag to a scale of 1 : 10.

9   Draw the flag to a scale of 1 : 5.

80 cm

110 cm

Let's investigate

Find the real area of the USA state flag shown above.
What is the area of the 1 : 10 scale drawing?
What do you notice?

Try this for other rectangles and 1 : 10 scale drawings of them.
What do you find?

What happens if you use a 1 : 5 scale?

Using a clinometer

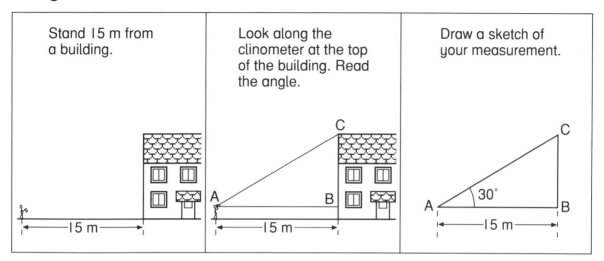

| Stand 15 m from a building. | Look along the clinometer at the top of the building. Read the angle. | Draw a sketch of your measurement. |

Calculating the height of a building

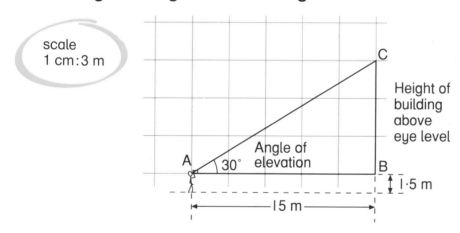

scale
1 cm : 3 m

Use squared paper.
Draw the horizontal distance AB to scale and
the angle of elevation.
The approximate height of the building can be found like this.

distance BC	9 m
height to eye	1·5 m
height of building	10·5 m

Use a clinometer to find the height of these.

1 a tall building   **2** a tree

The Statue of Liberty is 46 m high from the tip of the torch to the feet.

3 Stand in the same position and mark how tall you are.

4 About how many times taller than you is the Statue of Liberty?

5 Measure the length of your finger. If you were as tall as the Statue of Liberty, how long would your finger be?

6 Make a roll of paper to show it.

7 How long would your shoes need to be?

Let's investigate

Find the heights of some famous buildings.
Estimate how many floors they might have.
Work out how many times taller than you they are.

Number 4

A Make a pop-up page.

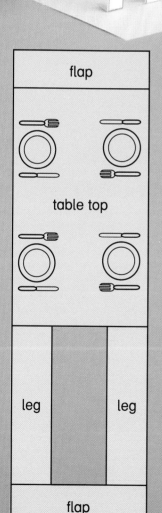

This line is 2 cm 3 mm long.
It is $2\frac{3}{10}$ cm or 2·3 cm.

Each centimetre on the ruler
is divided into 10 equal parts.
Each part is $\frac{1}{10}$ of a cm.
$\frac{1}{10}$ cm is called a millimetre.

Measure these.

1 Length of the table top is ☐ cm ☐ mm.
   This is ☐$\frac{☐}{10}$ cm or ☐ · ☐ cm.

2 Length of a leg is ☐ cm ☐ mm.
   This is ☐$\frac{☐}{10}$ cm or ☐ · ☐ cm.

3 Width of the table top is ☐ cm ☐ mm.
   This is ☐$\frac{☐}{10}$ cm or ☐ · ☐ cm.

4 What is the perimeter
   of the table top?

5 Measure the length and
   width of the rectangle
   you must cut out to
   make the pop-up table.

6 Draw the rectangle on stiff paper.
   What is its perimeter?

   Cut it out and make the pop-up table.

Fold a sheet of paper in half.

Mark on it where to
stick the flaps to
make the table pop-up.

Stick the flaps onto the paper.
Wait until they dry and fold the
paper to make a pop-up page.

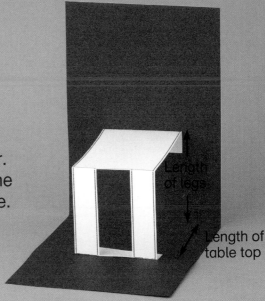

Length
of legs

Length of
table top

Pop-up chair

3·7 cm	3·1 cm	2·9 cm	1 cm
			flap
back	seat	legs	

7 Round each of the lengths and add them
to find the approximate length of card to
make a pop-up chair.

approximate length of   back ☐ cm
                        seat ☐ cm
                        legs ☐ cm
                        flap ☐ cm

approximate length needed ☐ cm

8 Draw the outline exactly on card.
Cut it out and complete your pop-up page.

Let's investigate

Design a card with a pop-up house.
Show your measurements in cm and mm.

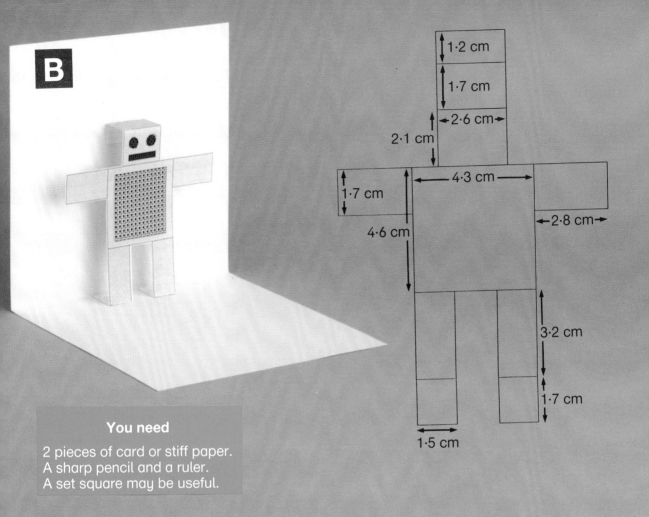

B

1·2 cm

1·7 cm

←2·6 cm→

2·1 cm

1·7 cm

←4·3 cm→

4·6 cm

←2·8 cm→

3·2 cm

1·7 cm

1·5 cm

You need

2 pieces of card or stiff paper.
A sharp pencil and a ruler.
A set square may be useful.

Make this fun pop-up card for a young child.
It can be for any occasion.

1   Round all the measurements.
    Add them to find the approximate length and
    width of card to make the robot.

2   Measure and draw the outline on a suitable piece of card or
    stiff paper.

3   Cut it out and fold the flaps.

4   Fold a sheet of card or stiff paper in half.

5   Add the actual robot measurements to find
    where to stick the head flap.

6   Stick the flaps onto the card.

$\frac{1}{10}$ of the pattern is red.

$\frac{1}{10} = 0.1$ This is a decimal fraction

whole ones tenths

7 $\frac{3}{10}$ or ☐·☐ of the pattern is blue.

8 $\frac{☐}{☐}$ or ☐·4 of the pattern is green.

9 $\frac{☐}{☐}$ or ☐·☐ of the pattern is yellow.

10 Colour a pattern on a hundred square. Write the decimal fraction for each colour.

Change these decimals to fractions.

11 0·7   **12** 0·1

13 0·6   **14** 0·5

15 0·2   **16** 0·4

17 0·9   **18** 0·8

Draw each of the shapes below.
Write as decimals the fraction of each that is coloured and the fraction that is not coloured.

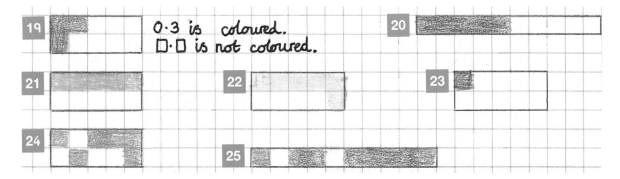

19   0·3 is coloured.
0·0 is not coloured.

20

21   **22**   **23**

24   **25**

0   0·5   1   2   3

26 Copy the number line and show these decimals on it.

0·9   2·7   1·3   0·7   1·8   2·2   2·0   1·1

27 Write them in order starting with the smallest.

How far away from 1 is each of the following decimals?

28 0·9   **29** 1·3   **30** 0·5   **31** 1.8   **32** 2.2

Write the smallest number in each of the following sets.

33 0·7 or 7   **34** 0·3 or 0·5   **35** 1·6 or 0·6

36 1·1, 0·1 or 1   **37** 0·8 or 1·2

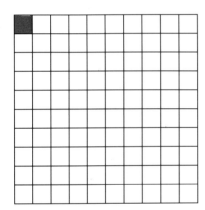

You need a 10 × 10 grid or a hundred square.
Colour one square red.
This is $\frac{1}{100}$ of the large square.

$$\frac{1}{100} = 0·01$$

whole ones tenths hundredths

38 Colour 7 squares purple.
This is $\frac{\square}{100}$ or $\square · \square\square$.

39 Colour 0·26 green, 0·12 black and 0·31 blue.
What decimal fraction of the whole grid is not coloured?

40 What are the decimal fractions
for $\frac{1}{4}$ and $\frac{3}{4}$ of the whole grid?

$\frac{1}{2}$ of the grid
is 0·50. We can
write this as 0·5.

Let's investigate

Find a fraction that will fit between $\frac{3}{4}$ and $\frac{4}{5}$.
Find as many as you can.

55

C

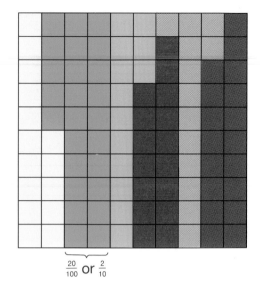

$\frac{20}{100}$ or $\frac{2}{10}$

$\frac{15}{100}$ of the pattern is yellow.

$\frac{15}{100} = \frac{10}{100} + \frac{5}{100}$

$\frac{15}{100} = \frac{1}{10} + \frac{5}{100}$

$\frac{15}{100} = 0.15$

1 Show the green squares as tenths and hundredths.

$\frac{2}{10} + \frac{5}{100} = \frac{25}{100} = 0.\square\square$

Show these in the same way.

2 the blue squares   **3** the red squares

4 the orange squares   **5** the purple squares

6 Write the following decimals as fractions.

0.01   0.02   0.03

7 Draw a number line.

```
0                    0.1                    0.2
└─┴─┴─┴─┴─┴─┴─┴─┴─┴─┴─┴─┴─┴─┴─┴─┴─┴─┴─┴─┴─┘
```

Mark on the following numbers.

0.12   0.17   0.03   0.11   0.08

Round the following numbers to 1 place after the decimal point.

0.32 → 0.3   0.37 → 0.4

8 0.17   **9** 0.12   **10** 0.11

11 2.48   **12** 4.23   **13** 15.08

14 Use a calculator.

$\frac{3}{4} = 3 \div 4 = \square . \square\square = \frac{\square\square}{100}$

$\frac{6}{8} = \square \div \square = \square . \square\square = \frac{\square\square}{100}$

$\frac{9}{12} = \square \div \square = \square . \square\square = \frac{\square\square}{100}$

Explain what you find.

15 Use your calculator to change these fractions to decimals and then put them in order, largest first.

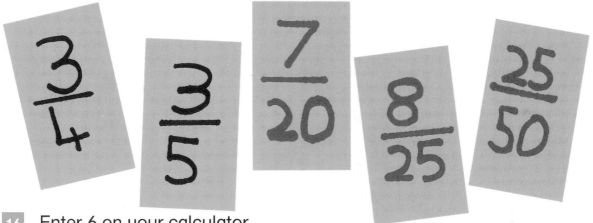

16 Enter 6 on your calculator.
Divide it by 10.
Divide by 10 again.
Keep on dividing by 10 and record your result each time.

	Number	÷ 10	÷ 100	÷ 1000
Fraction	6	$\frac{6}{10}$	$\frac{6}{100}$	
Decimal	6	0·6	0·06	

17 Try it with other starting numbers and record your results.

Let's investigate

Find the largest fraction you can that is less than $\frac{1}{2}$.

Show it as a decimal.

ordinates

A **Journey to Planet Marlon**

One   day Captain Valiant set off
for the   mysterious   planet Marlon.

Remember to read the horizontal axis first.

1 Copy the first grid.
Join the co-ordinates to draw Captain Valiant.

Start at (1, 0) → (3, 3) → (2, 7) → (1, 9) → (7, 10) → (6, 9)
→ (8, 8) → (7, 8) → (7, 6) → (8, 5) → (7, 5) → (6, 3)
→ (5, 2) → (3, 3)

Join (5, 2) to (7, 0).

Draw the eye, hair and the mouth.

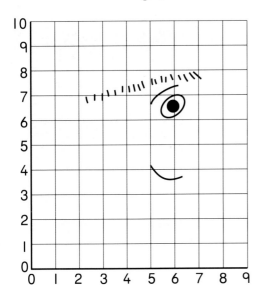

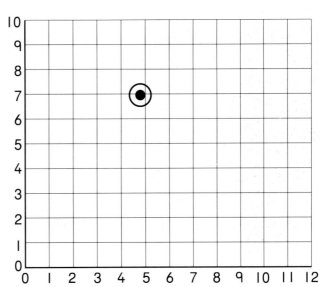

She   took   her parrot for company.

2 Copy the second grid.
Join the co-ordinates to draw the parrot.

(5, 0) → (6, 1) → (5, 4) → (3, 6) → (2, 5) → (2, 4) → (1, 5)
→ (2, 7) → (4, 9) → (7, 9) → (6, 8) → (7, 8) → (6, 7)
→ (8, 7) → (7, 6) → (10, 4) → (12, 0)

3 Plan the co-ordinates for the parrot's pot of seeds.
Make it an interesting shape.
Draw it on the grid.

They went to the launch pad
and boarded their spaceship.
They took their exploring kit with them.

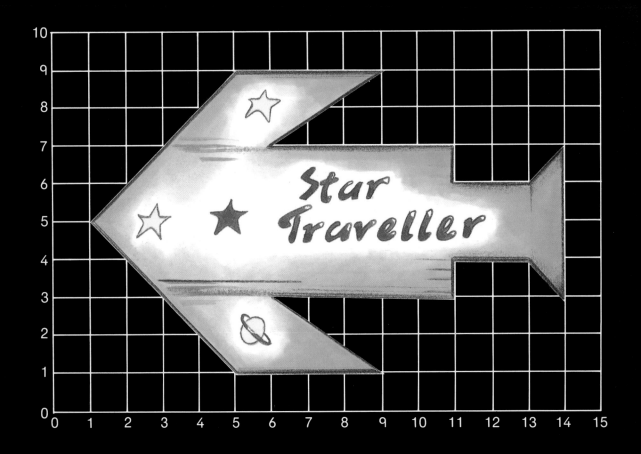

4   Write the co-ordinates of the vertices of Star Traveller.

5   Design your own spaceship.
Write the co-ordinates of its vertices.

6   Work with a friend and make a list of the
things that could have been in the exploring kit.

Captain Valiant and her parrot steered their spaceship through the planets and stars to reach planet Marlon.

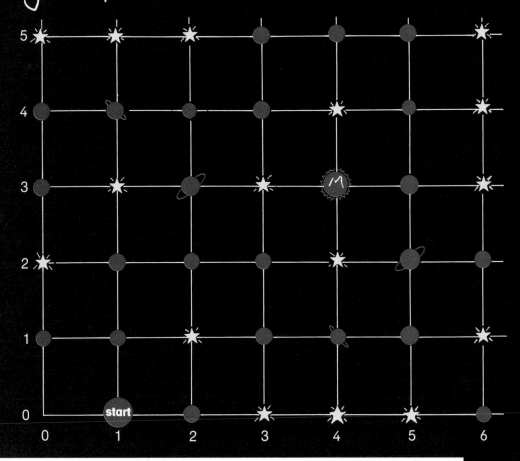

They travelled from planet to planet along the grid lines from (1, 0) to Planet Marlon. They did not visit any stars.

7   Find two routes. Write the co-ordinates for each of the planets on their shorter route.

8   Do the same for the longer route.

Let's investigate

Look at the co-ordinates of the planets.
Reverse their numbers, which ones still show a planet?

Do the same for the stars. What do you discover?

aptain Valiant was on a quest to find a ery rare and beautiful crystal found only on Planet Marlon. When the two intrepid explorers landed they found a plan of part of the planet.

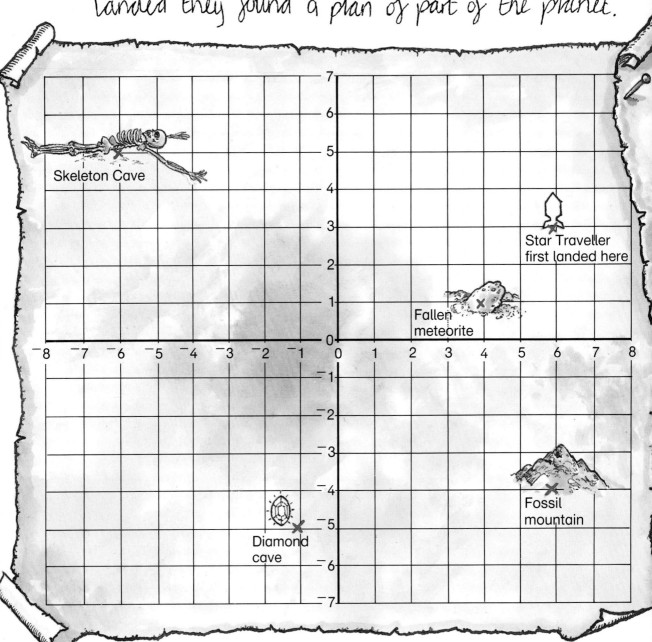

Skeleton Cave

Star Traveller first landed here

Fallen meteorite

Diamond cave

Fossil mountain

You still need to read the horizontal axis first each time.

These instructions were pinned to the plan. Captain Valiant and the parrot followed them and arrived at the Silver Dust Pit.

Fly to the Space Observatory at (3, 6). Collect a galaxy telescope.

Fly to the ruined Spacecraft at (⁻4, 3). Collect a Marlon route finder.

Now go to the disused crystal mine at (⁻5, ⁻2). Collect a book about the Marlon crystal.

Lastly fly to the Silver Dust Pit at (2, ⁻3). Collect a silver casket for the crystal. Inside the casket are your next instructions.

1 Write the co-ordinates of Star Traveller's first landing place.

2 Copy the grid and mark on it each of the places that Captain Valiant had to visit.

3 Write the co-ordinates of each of the other places shown on the plan.

4 Make up the names of 4 other places on Planet Marlon.
Mark their positions on the grid, putting them in different quadrants.
Write the name and co-ordinates of each one.

> A quadrant is one of the four parts of the grid.

5 Draw each of the 4 places and write about something that happened at each of them in the past.

Let's investigate

Following the instructions in the casket the explorers flew on to Pumice Pinnacle. Here they found another note and a different plan.

You must travel on foot to reach the Crystal Vault.

DO NOT CROSS THE MOLTEN LAVA LAKE.

Rules for using the plan
1 You must travel along grid lines.
2 You must not travel more than 3 squares without changing direction.

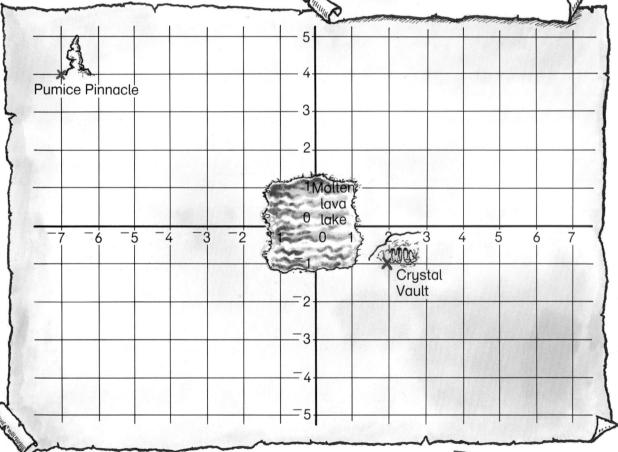

Copy the grid.
Find 3 ways for Captain Valiant to reach the vault.
For each route write the co-ordinates of each change of direction.
Which is the shortest route you can find?

C Captain Valiant found these instructions pinned to the door of the vault.

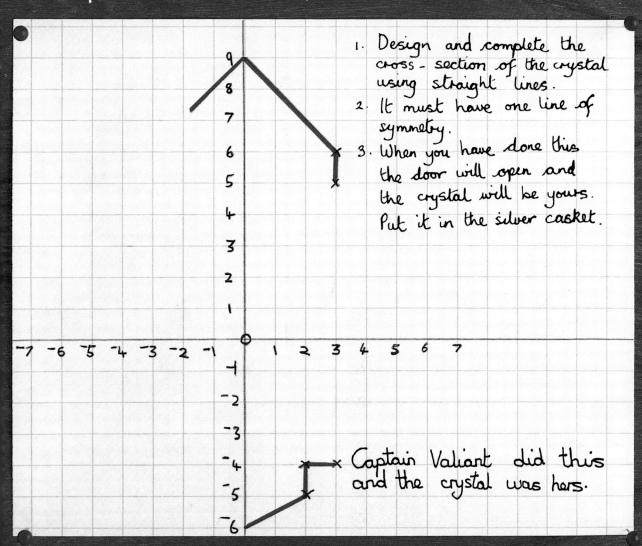

1. Design and complete the cross-section of the crystal using straight lines.
2. It must have one line of symmetry.
3. When you have done this the door will open and the crystal will be yours. Put it in the silver casket.

Captain Valiant did this and the crystal was hers.

1 Draw the cross-section of the crystal on a grid. Write the co-ordinates of the vertices.

Let's investigate

Use 2 dice and a grid showing 4 quadrants.
Design a co-ordinate game for 2 or more players.

Data 3

A   The school band went on a trip to France and Germany.

Diary	
8 a.m.	Set off by coach. Travelled the 55 miles to Dover at a steady speed.
9 a.m.	Arrived at Dover.
9:30 a.m.	Ferry set off from Dover. It sailed for 22 miles at a steady speed.
11 a.m.	Ferry docked at Calais.

1   Copy and complete the table for the journey.

Time	8 a.m.	9 a.m.	9:30 a.m.	11 a.m.
Distance travelled in miles	0		55	

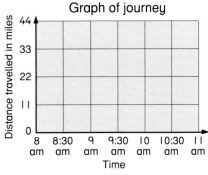

Graph of journey

2   Draw a line graph to show the journey.

3   Copy and complete this line graph of the ferry's journey from Dover to Calais.

4   A hovercraft sets off at 9:30 a.m. and takes 40 minutes for the same trip. It travels at a steady speed. Show this journey on the same graph.

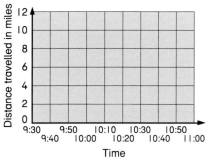

5   Why is one graph steeper than the other?

Let's investigate

Draw graphs to show different ways that you might travel to school. Explain them.

B

The children used a graph to work out how many French francs and German marks they would get for their English pounds.

Exchange rates can change each day.

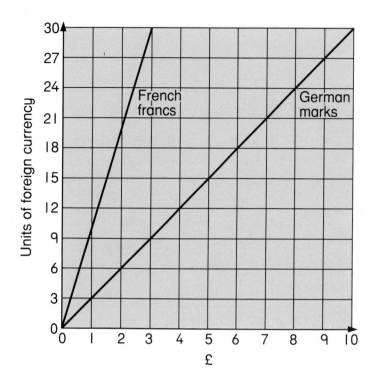

Units of foreign currency vs £

Approximately how many French francs would you get for the following amounts?

1 £3   2 £1   3 £6   4 £10

Approximately how many German marks would you get for the following amounts?

5 £10   6 £6   7 £4   8 £1

Approximately how many pounds would you get for the following amounts?

9 15 marks   10 45 marks   11 20 francs   12 60 francs

Let's investigate

Find exchange rates for the pound in other currencies.
Round the exchange rates to the nearest whole number when appropriate. Record your findings.
Write some questions about the exchange rates for a friend.

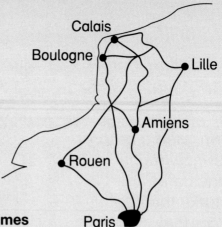

C

The children's coach drove
from Calais to Paris.

Distance chart and approximate driving times

	Amiens	Boulogne	Calais	Lille	Paris	Rouen
Amiens	–	123 km 1 hr 45	155 km 2 hr 10	115 km 1 hr 30	148 km 1 hr 45	113 km 1 hr 45
Boulogne	123 km 1 hr 45	–	34 km 0 hr 35	115 km 1 hr 40	243 km 3 hr 35	177 km 2 hr 35
Calais	155 km 2 hr 10	34 km 0 hr 35	–	112 km 1 hr 20		218 km 3 hr 05
Lille	115 km 1 hr 30	115 km 1 hr 40	112 km 1 hr 20	–	219 km 2 hr 25	218 km 3 hr 15
Paris	148 km 1 hr 45	243 km 3 hr 35		219 km 2 hr 25	–	139 km 1 hr 40
Rouen	113 km 1 hr 45	177 km 2 hr 35	218 km 3 hr 05	218 km 3 hr 15	139 km 1 hr 40	–

Use the two-way table and the map.
Find the distance in km for the following routes.

1. Calais → Amiens → Paris
2. Calais → Lille → Paris
3. Calais → Boulogne → Paris
4. Calais → Rouen → Paris
5. Which of these is the quickest route? Calais → —— → Paris
6. Suggest reasons why the quickest route is not the shortest.

Let's investigate

Ask 10 children which two capital cities in Europe they
would most like to visit.
Record their answers in a two-way table. Write about it.

68

A

There are 24 cars on a stall.
How many cars would a person have if she bought the following?

1 $\frac{1}{2}$ of them   **2** $\frac{3}{4}$ of them   **3** $\frac{1}{3}$ of them   **4** $\frac{5}{8}$ of them

There are 100 cards.
How many are sold if a
person buys the following?

5 $\frac{1}{2}$ **6** $\frac{1}{4}$ **7** $\frac{1}{10}$ **8** $\frac{7}{10}$

9 50%   **10** 25%

11 75%   **12** 100%

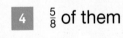

10% of
100 is 10.

13 80%   **14** 40%

15 15%   **16** 35%

17 45%   **18** 62%

What fraction of the 18 cakes are the following?

19 cherry   **20** cream   **21** chocolate

Make fraction charts to help with the following.

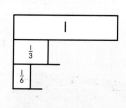

22 $\frac{3}{4} = \frac{\square}{8}$ **23** $\frac{3}{5} = \frac{\square}{10}$

24 $\frac{4}{8} = \frac{\square}{2}$ **25** $\frac{4}{6} = \frac{\square}{3}$

26 $\frac{1}{3} + \frac{1}{3} = \frac{\square}{3}$ **27** $\frac{2}{6} + \frac{3}{6} = \frac{\square}{6}$

28 $\frac{1}{2} + \frac{1}{2} = \square$ **29** $\frac{5}{8} + \frac{2}{8} = \frac{\square}{8}$

30 $\frac{3}{4} - \frac{1}{4} = \frac{\square}{4}$ **31** $\frac{7}{8} - \frac{3}{8} = \frac{\square}{8}$

32 $\frac{4}{10} - \frac{3}{10} = \frac{\square}{10}$ **33** $\frac{9}{10} - \frac{5}{10} = \frac{\square}{10}$

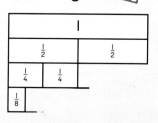
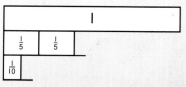

Let's investigate

A tray of cakes can be divided exactly in $\frac{1}{2}$ or $\frac{1}{3}$ or $\frac{1}{4}$.

How many cakes are on the tray?

Find different numbers of cakes less than 100.

Do the same for $\frac{1}{2}, \frac{1}{5}, \frac{1}{10}$.

70

B This table shows the number of stamps in a stamp collection.

Country	Number of stamps
Polish	100
French	20
Jamaican	50
Indian	25
Mexican	☐
Total 200	

1 How many Mexican stamps are there?

What fraction of the total stamps are the following?

2 Polish   **3** French   **4** Jamaican   **5** Indian

Add these fractions

6 $\frac{1}{2} + \frac{1}{4} = \frac{\square}{\square}$ **7** $\frac{1}{2} + \frac{3}{8} = \frac{\square}{\square}$ **8** $\frac{1}{5} + \frac{3}{10} = \frac{\square}{\square}$

9 $\frac{1}{2} + \frac{1}{3} = \frac{\square}{\square}$ **10** $\frac{1}{2} + \frac{1}{5} = \frac{\square}{\square}$ **11** $\frac{1}{2} + \frac{1}{10} = \frac{\square}{\square}$

Use a calculator to find the following amounts.

12 $\frac{3}{5}$ of 270 m   **13** $\frac{3}{4}$ of 144 m

14 $\frac{1}{10}$ of 3 m   **15** $\frac{2}{5}$ of £135

16 $\frac{3}{4}$ of £5·24   **17** $\frac{3}{10}$ of £14·50

18 20% of £65   **19** 5% of £40

20 15% of £640   **21** 6% of £54

22 3% of £248   **23** 8% of £906

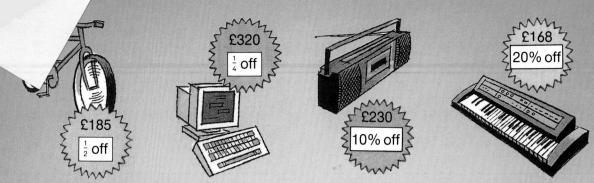

24 How much is saved altogether by buying the items shown above in the sale?

Let's investigate

Share £100 into 3 different amounts.
Show the amounts as percentages of £100.

£ ☐ + £ ☐ + £ ☐ = £100

☐% + ☐% + ☐% = 100%

Find different ways to do it.
Explain what you discover.

C Find the actual cost of the following sale items.

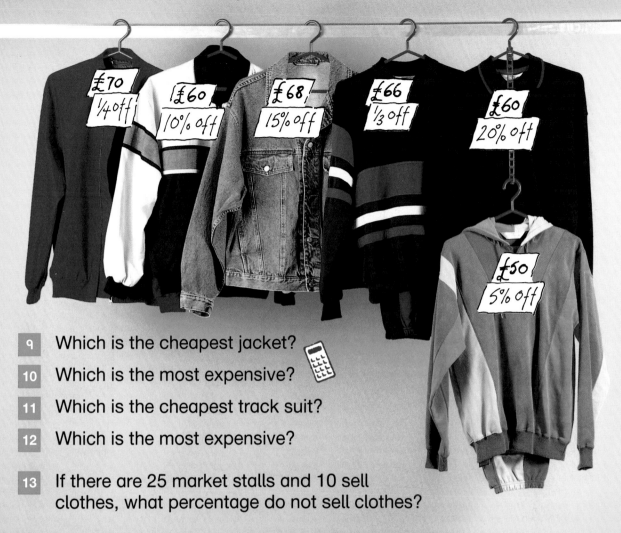

9. Which is the cheapest jacket?

10. Which is the most expensive?

11. Which is the cheapest track suit?

12. Which is the most expensive?

13. If there are 25 market stalls and 10 sell clothes, what percentage do not sell clothes?

Which of these amounts of money would you rather have?

14. 20% of £20 or 30% of £15

15. 25% of £30 or 15% of £51

Change these fractions to percentages

16. $\frac{3}{10} = \Box$%

17. $\frac{9}{10}$

18. $\frac{1}{4}$

19. $\frac{3}{5}$

20. $\frac{19}{20}$

21. $\frac{14}{25}$

22. $\frac{1}{8}$

23. $\frac{3}{8}$

Let's investigate

Find different fractions that will change into 50%.
What do you notice about the fractions?
Do the same for 25% and 75%.

Number 6

A   Detective work

1   Which rectangles have the same areas?
How did you find your answers?

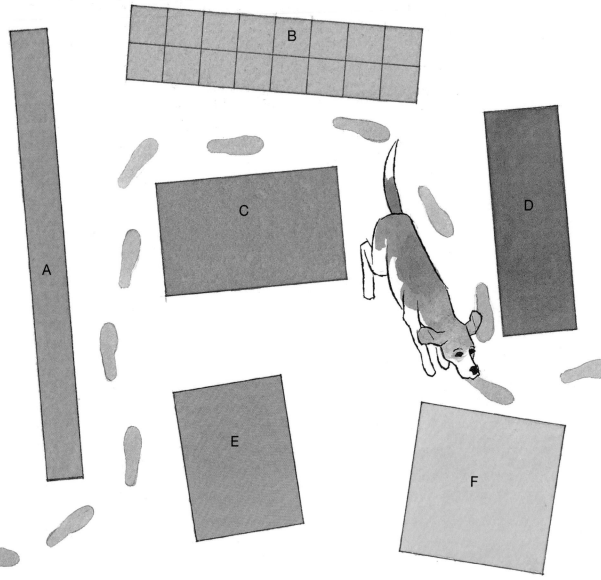

2   Which rectangles have the same perimeters?
Explain how you found your answers.

Which pairs have the same volume?
Show how you found your answers.

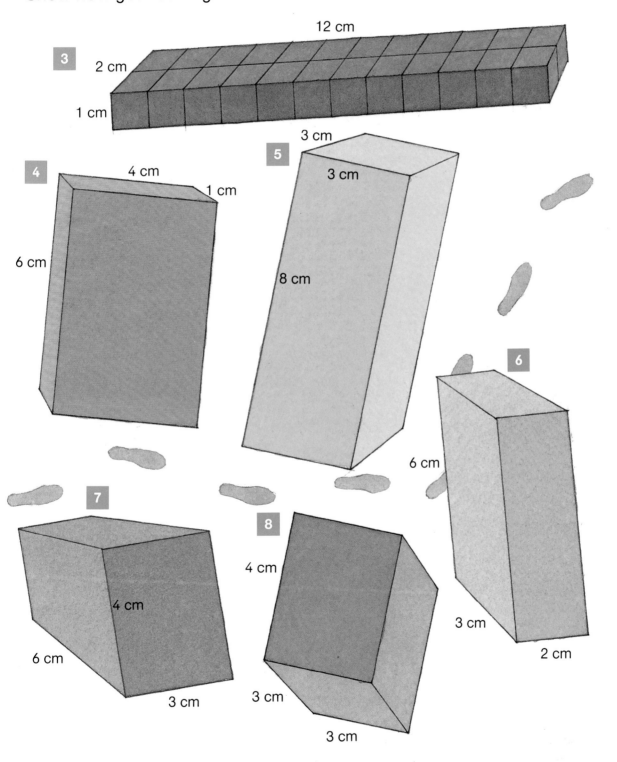

12 cm

3

2 cm

1 cm

3 cm

5

3 cm

8 cm

4

4 cm

1 cm

6 cm

6

6 cm

7

4 cm

6 cm

3 cm

8

4 cm

3 cm

3 cm

3 cm

2 cm

9 Put in the missing information.

$20 \text{ cm}^2 = 5 \text{ cm} \times \square \text{ cm}$

10

Find another rectangle with the same area.

$\square \text{ cm}^2 = \square \text{ cm} \times \square \text{ cm}$

11 Give the length and width of 4 different rectangles with areas of 30 cm².

Let's investigate

Find at least 5 different rectangles that have the same area.

Record your results.

76

B A spy used a code to show the perimeter of a square.

Perimeter = length + length + length + length

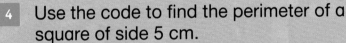

$p = l + l + l + l$

or $p = 4l$

This is called a formula for the perimeter of a square of side l.

1 What do you think p stands for?

2 What do you think l stands for?

3 What do you think $4l$ stands for?

4 Use the code to find the perimeter of a square of side 5 cm.

5 Use the spy's code to write a way of finding the perimeter of this triangle.

$p =$

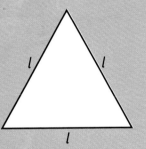

The spy often uses different letters.
Use a code to write ways of finding the perimeters of these shapes.

6
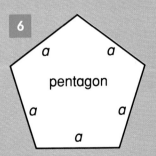
pentagon

7
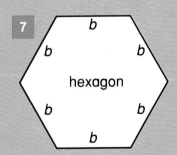
hexagon

8
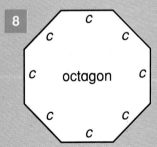
octagon

9 If the sides of the pentagon are 3 cm, what is the perimeter?

10 If the sides of the octagon are 5 cm, what is the perimeter?

11 If the perimeter of the hexagon is 24 cm, how long is each side?

Write a formula for the perimeter of each of these shapes.

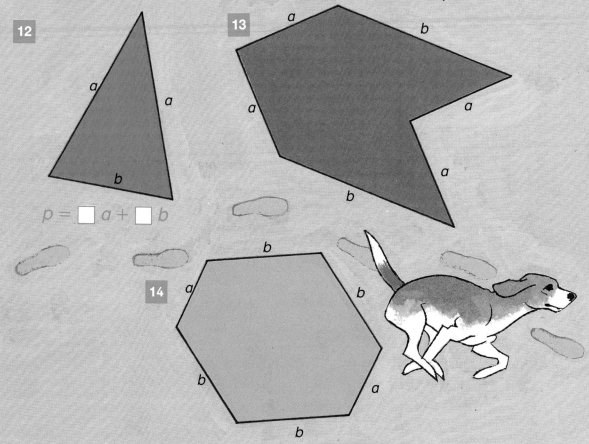

12

$$p = \boxed{}\, a + \boxed{}\, b$$

13

14

15 Complete the formula for finding the perimeter of this rectangle.

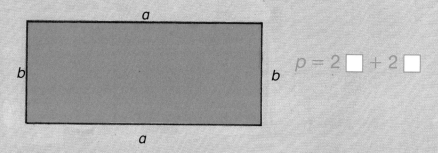

$$p = 2\,\boxed{} + 2\,\boxed{}$$

16 If the sides of a rectangle are 2 cm and 5 cm, what is the perimeter?

17 If the perimeter of a rectangle is 18 cm, what could *a* and *b* be?

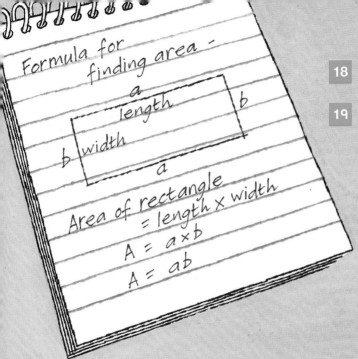

Formula for finding area –

Area of rectangle
= length × width

$A = a \times b$

$A = ab$

18 What does *A* stand for?

19 What does *ab* stand for?

What is the formula for area of the following 2 shapes?

20
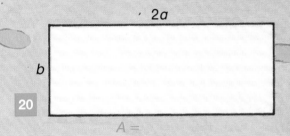
2a

b

A =

21
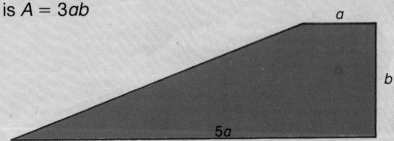
a

2b

22 The formula for the area of this shape
is $A = 3ab$

a

b

5a

What is the area if *a* = 2 cm and *b* = 3 cm?

Let's investigate

Draw some shapes that fit this formula
for finding their perimeters.

$p = 3a + 2b$

C

Write a formula for the following.

1. How many rolls in a number of packets?
   Explain what each letter and number you use means.

2. Do the same to show how many yogurts in a number of packs.

3. Write a formula for the perimeter of the triangle.

4. If b is 3, what is the perimeter?

5. If the perimeter is 15 cm, what is b?

b cm   *b* cm

1 cm

Let's investigate

Try to find a length for *a* so that the square has an area of 3 cm².

Use a calculator to try different values for *a*.

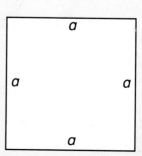

a

a

a

a

Angles 2

Look at the diagram.
Choose the correct word
for these sentences.

vertical
perpendicular
horizontal
parallel

1. The red lines are _____

2. The yellow lines are _____

3. The blue and green lines are _____

4. The red and yellow lines are _____

5. If the blue line is vertical, the green line is _____

6. Draw two different 4 sided shapes each with one
   pair of parallel sides.

Measure and name the angles in the following patterns. Copy and complete each table.

7

angle	name
$a = \square °$	acute
b	
c	
d	

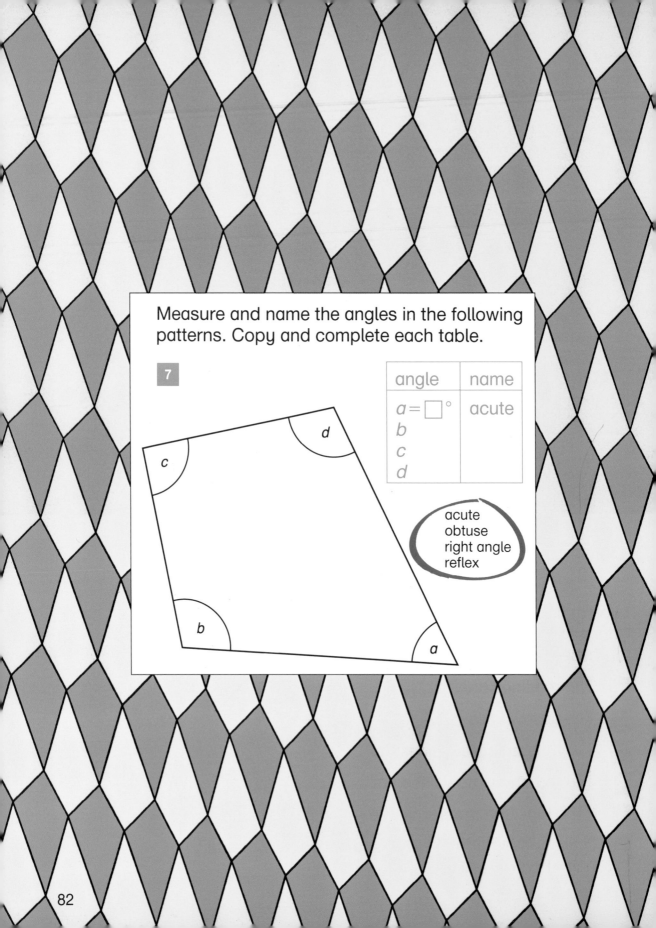

acute
obtuse
right angle
reflex

8

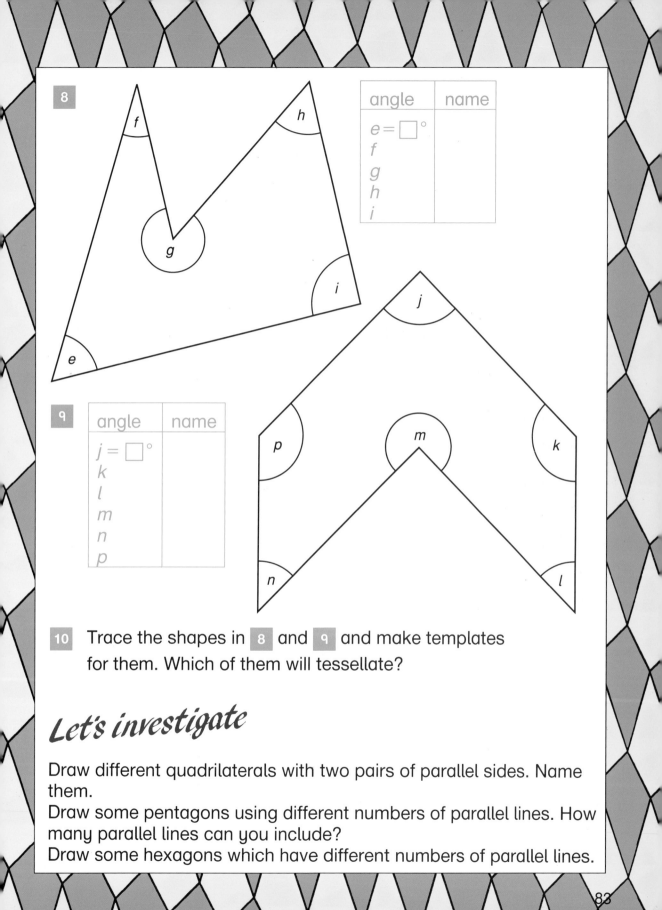

angle	name
$e = \square°$	
f	
g	
h	
i	

9

angle	name
$j = \square°$	
k	
l	
m	
n	
p	

10 Trace the shapes in **8** and **9** and make templates for them. Which of them will tessellate?

Let's investigate

Draw different quadrilaterals with two pairs of parallel sides. Name them.

Draw some pentagons using different numbers of parallel lines. How many parallel lines can you include?

Draw some hexagons which have different numbers of parallel lines.

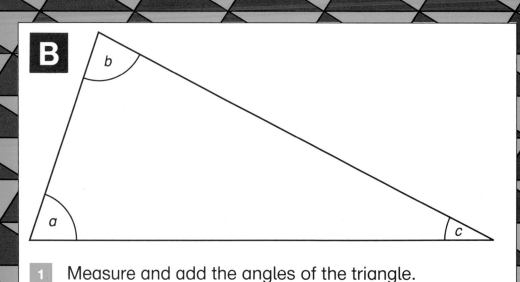

B

1 Measure and add the angles of the triangle.

$\square^\circ + \square^\circ + \square^\circ = \square^\circ$

What do you notice?

Draw the following triangles using the measurements given. Measure the lettered angles.

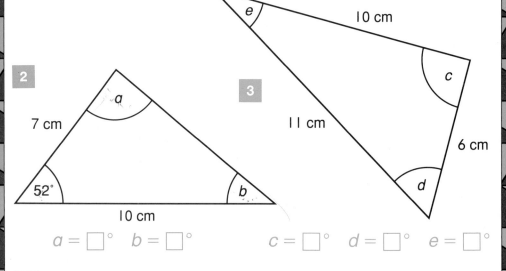

2

7 cm

52°

10 cm

3

11 cm

10 cm

6 cm

$a = \square^\circ \quad b = \square^\circ \qquad c = \square^\circ \quad d = \square^\circ \quad e = \square^\circ$

4 Draw 2 different triangles each with one side 10 cm long. Measure and add the angles of each triangle. Explain what you find.

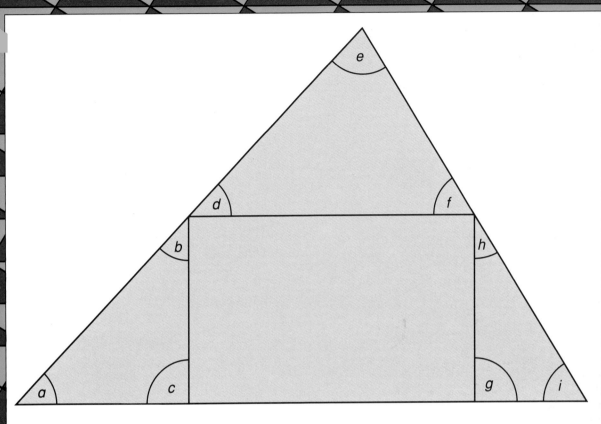

5   Measure all the angles of the three small triangles.
    How many pairs of equal angles are there altogether?

Let's investigate

Draw a large triangle.
Mark the centres of the
sides and join them up.
Measure all the angles of
the 4 small triangles.
What do you notice?
Does this work with other triangles?

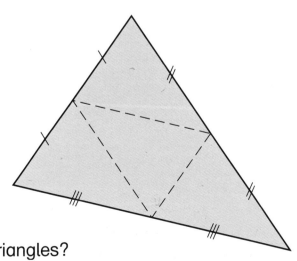

C

1 Use templates to draw all 4 shapes. Measure the angles of each one. Copy and complete the table.

shape	each angle
square	
equilateral triangle	
regular hexagon	
regular octagon	

2 Use the templates to make the following patterns. The length of each side of all the templates must be the same.

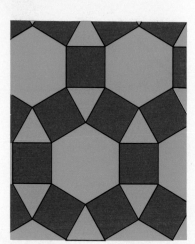

Use your table. Add the angles at a point on each of the designs.

3 octagon + square + octagon = ☐°.

4 hexagon + triangle + hexagon + triangle = ☐°

5 hexagon + square + triangle + square = ☐°

6 What do you notice about the angles at a point? Explain why each group of shapes tessellate together.

7 Use card to make this quadrilateral template.
Use the measurements given.

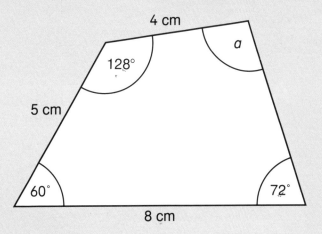

8 Measure the missing angle.

$a = \boxed{}°$

9 Add all the angles together.

$72° + 60° + 128° + a° = \boxed{}°$

Use your card template. Draw and cut out 8 identical quadrilaterals from paper.
Mark the angles a, b, c, d on each quadrilateral.
Make the 8 quadrilaterals tessellate.

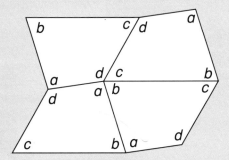

10 What do you notice about the angles at a point?

11 Why does this quadrilateral tessellate?

12 Try this again with another quadrilateral.

Let's investigate

Draw a quadrilateral of any shape.
Draw one diagonal to divide it
into 2 triangles.
What will be the sum of
the angles $a + b + c + d + e + f$?
Will it work for all quadrilaterals?

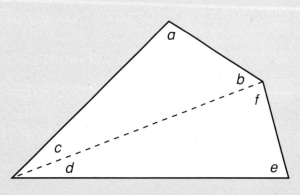

A These are some of the highest mountains and longest rivers on Planet Earth.

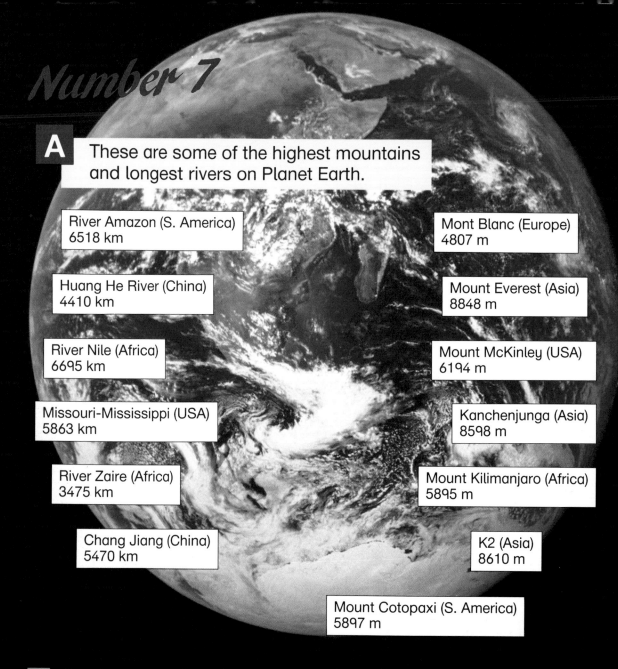

River Amazon (S. America)
6518 km

Mont Blanc (Europe)
4807 m

Huang He River (China)
4410 km

Mount Everest (Asia)
8848 m

River Nile (Africa)
6695 km

Mount McKinley (USA)
6194 m

Missouri-Mississippi (USA)
5863 km

Kanchenjunga (Asia)
8598 m

River Zaire (Africa)
3475 km

Mount Kilimanjaro (Africa)
5895 m

Chang Jiang (China)
5470 km

K2 (Asia)
8610 m

Mount Cotopaxi (S. America)
5897 m

1 Write the rivers in order of length, shortest first.

2 Write the mountains in order of height, highest first.

What is the difference in height between these mountains?

3 Mount Everest and Kanchenjunga.

4 Mount McKinley and K2.

5 How much longer is the River Nile than the River Zaire?

6 How much shorter is the Chang Jiang than the River Amazon?

Name the numbered planets.
The diameters will help you.

14 If the Earth were the size of a marble which planets would be the size of a tennis ball and a football?

15 Round these diameters to the nearest thousand km. Mars Venus Earth Mercury

16 Which planet is approximately 7 times bigger than Mars in diameter?

17 Estimate the difference between the diameters of Mars and Mercury. Find the real answer on a calculator.

Diameters of the planets	
Mercury	4878 km
Venus	12 100 km
Earth	12 756 km
Mars	6786 km
Jupiter	143 000 km
Saturn	120 500 km
Uranus	51 100 km
Neptune	49 500 km
Pluto	about 2300 km

You need a calculator.

Mars has a diameter of nearly 7000 km.

18 Find the missing numbers.
7000 → ☐ Tens
7000 → ☐ Hundreds
7000 → ☐ Thousands

Record your answers each time.

19 What do you notice about these numbers?
30 Hundreds
3 Thousands
300 Tens

20 Enter 6 on your calculator.
Change 6 to 60 in 1 move by multiplying.
Change 60 to 600 in 1 move by multiplying.
Change 600 to 6000 in 1 move by multiplying.

21 Make zero
Enter 2483.
Change all the digits to zero.
Do it in 3 subtractions.
Do it in 2 subtractions.

The river Zaire is 3475 km long.

22 Enter 3475 on your calculator.
Change 3475 to 3575 in 1 move.
Change 3575 to 6575 in 1 move.
Change 6575 to 6595 in 1 move.
Change 6595 to 6695 in 1 move.

The river Nile is 6695 km long.

23 Find the missing numbers.
$2 \times 50 = \square$
$2 \times 100 = \square$
$2 \times 200 = \square$
Find the pattern.
Predict these answers.
$2 \times 400 = \square$
$2 \times 800 = \square$
Check using your calculator.

24 I multiply a number
by 10, then by 100.
The answer is 12 000.
What was the number?

25 Times 10
How many times do you
think you will have to press
$\boxed{\times}\boxed{10}$ to change 10 into 100 000?
Check on your calculator.

26
$99 + 99 = \square$
$99 + 99 + 99 = \square$
$99 + 99 + 99 + 99 = \square$
Find the pattern and predict the
next 3 lines.
Check using your calculator.

27 It takes Mercury 88 days to orbit the sun.
Estimate how many orbits it will make in 8800 days.
Check using your calculator.

B The diameter of the sun is over 1 million km.

1 million is 1 000 000 or one thousand thousands.

A short way of writing 10×10 is 10^2 or 10 to the power of 2. $10 \times 10 \times 10$ is 10^3 or 10 to the power of 3

1 Copy and complete the pattern up to 1 million.

$$
\begin{array}{lll}
10 = 10 & = 10^1 \\
100 = 10 \times 10 & = 10^2 \\
1000 = 10 \times 10 \times 10 & = 10^3 \\
10\ 000 = & = 10^\square \\
100\ 000 = & = 10^\square \\
1\ 000\ 000 = & = \square^\square
\end{array}
$$

Use a calculator to complete the following patterns.

2
$$
\begin{array}{l}
1 \times 100 = \square = 10^2 \\
10 \times 100 = \square = 10^\square \\
100 \times 100 = \square = 10^\square \\
1000 \times 100 = \square = 10^\square \\
10\ 000 \times 100 = \square = 10^\square
\end{array}
$$

3
$$
\begin{array}{l}
1 \times 1000 = \square = 10^3 \\
10 \times 1000 = \square = 10^\square \\
100 \times 1000 = \square = 10^\square \\
1000 \times 1000 = \square = 10^\square
\end{array}
$$

4 What do you notice about the number of 0s and the index number in the patterns?

10^5 — This is the index number or power number.

5 Find an object that is 1 cm across.
Find something that is approximately 10 times bigger or 10^1 cm.

6 Copy and complete the chart. Suggest things that are the approximate lengths.

Length	Object
10^1 cm	10 cm
10^2 cm	$\square$ cm or $\square$ m
10^3 cm	$\square$ m
10^4 cm	$\square$ m
10^5 cm	$\square$ m or $\square$ km

7 What is 10^7 cm in km?
Can you think of anything that may be about 10^7 cm?

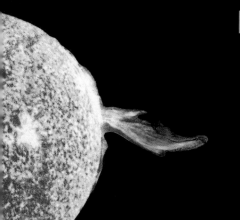

8 An unscrupulous space agent advertises voyages into space. He charges

for one day £2
double for two days £4
double for three days £8
and so on.

How much would the minimum 2 week holiday cost?

9 Complete the pattern of 2s

$2^1 = 2$
$2^2 = 2 \times 2 = 4$
$2^3 = 2 \times 2 \times 2 = \square$
$2^4 = 2 \times 2 \times 2 \times 2 = \square$
$2^5 = 2 \times 2 \times 2 \times 2 \times 2 = \square$
$2^6 = 2 \times 2 \times 2 \times 2 \times 2 \times 2 = \square$

10 Explain what you notice about the pattern of 2s.

Copy and complete these patterns.

11
$3^2 = 3 \times 3 = 9$
$3^3 = 3 \times 3 \times 3 = \square$
$3^4 = \qquad = \square$
$3^5 = \qquad = \square$

12
$5^2 = 5 \times 5 = \square$
$5^3 = \qquad = \square$
$5^4 = \qquad = \square$
$5^5 = \qquad = \square$

What do you notice about the last 2 digits each time?

13
$1^2 = \quad 1 \times \quad 1 = \square$
$11^2 = \quad 11 \times \quad 11 = \square$
$111^2 = 111 \times 111 = \square$

What do you notice about the pattern. Predict the answer to 1111^2

14 Which do you think will be bigger, 4^6 or 6^4? Check your prediction.

Find the missing numbers.

15 $\square^3 = 343$ **16** $\square^3 = 216$ **17** $\square^3 = 729$

18 When you double the length of the sides of a cube how much bigger does the volume get?

93

In 1682 Halley's comet was observed by Edmund Halley.

①⑥82 – The ① is the most important figure in 1682 as it is worth 1000. The ⑥ is the second most important figure as it is worth 600.
1682 is nearer to 1700 than to 1600 so when it is rounded to 2 significant figures, or the 2 most important figures, it is rounded up to 1700.

19 Round these dates to 2 significant figures.

Planet Uranus discovered	1781
Telescope invented	1608
Planet Neptune discovered	1846
Royal Greenwich Observatory founded	1675

Remember 5 always rounds up.

River	Amazon	Zaire	Huang He	Nile	Chang Jiang	Mississippi
Length	6518 km	3475 km	4410 km	6695 km	5470 km	3779 km

20 Find 2 of the rivers with a difference in length of 2285 km. First round the lengths to 2 significant figures to find the most likely pairs.

The first manned space flight was in 1961.
If this date is rounded to 3 significant figures it is nearer 1960 than 1970 so it is rounded down to 1960.

21 Round some historical dates, for example 1066, to 3 significant figures.

Let's investigate

Find pairs of numbers. The total for each pair must be 1800 when rounded to 2 significant figures.

Find pairs of numbers. The total for each pair must be 1990 when rounded to 3 significant figures.

C *This pattern has a constant difference of 2.*

1 $\underbrace{}_{2}$ 3 $\underbrace{}_{2}$ 5 $\underbrace{}_{2}$ 7 $\underbrace{}_{2}$ 9 $\underbrace{}_{2}$ 11 $\underbrace{}_{2}$ 13

difference → 2 2 2 2 2 2

Copy and complete the following patterns.

1	13	17	21	☐	29	33	☐	41
2	15	26	37	☐	59	70	☐	92
3	127	118	109	☐	☐	82	☐	
4	12	23	34	45	☐	☐	☐	89
5	234	345	456	☐	☐	789		
6	987	876	765	☐	☐	432		

7 Make up a pattern of your own for a friend to try.

In this pattern the second difference is 2 each time.

3 __ 5 __ 9 __ 15 __ 23 __ 33

first difference 2 __ 4 __ 6 __ 8 __ 10
second difference 2 2 2 2

Copy and complete the following patterns as above.

8	6	8	12	18	☐	☐	☐	62
9	3	6	11	18	☐	☐	☐	66
10	100	97	92	85	☐	☐	☐	37

Explain what is happening in these patterns.

11	1	2	3	5	8	13	21	34		
12	6	7	9	7	12	7	15	7	18	7	21

Let's investigate

Find as many ways as possible of completing this pattern.

1 2 4 ☐ ☐ ☐ ☐

95

Measurement 2

A

1. Shuffle a pack of cards.
   Time yourself to see
   how quickly you can
   sort them into sets
   or groups.

2. Shuffle the cards and do the same again.
   Compare your times.

3. How long do you think it will take you to
   make this pattern using counters?
   The counters must be touching.

4. Do it and time yourself.
   Were you slower or quicker
   than your estimated time?

Estimate these measurements
in metres or centimetres.
Find ways to check your
estimates.

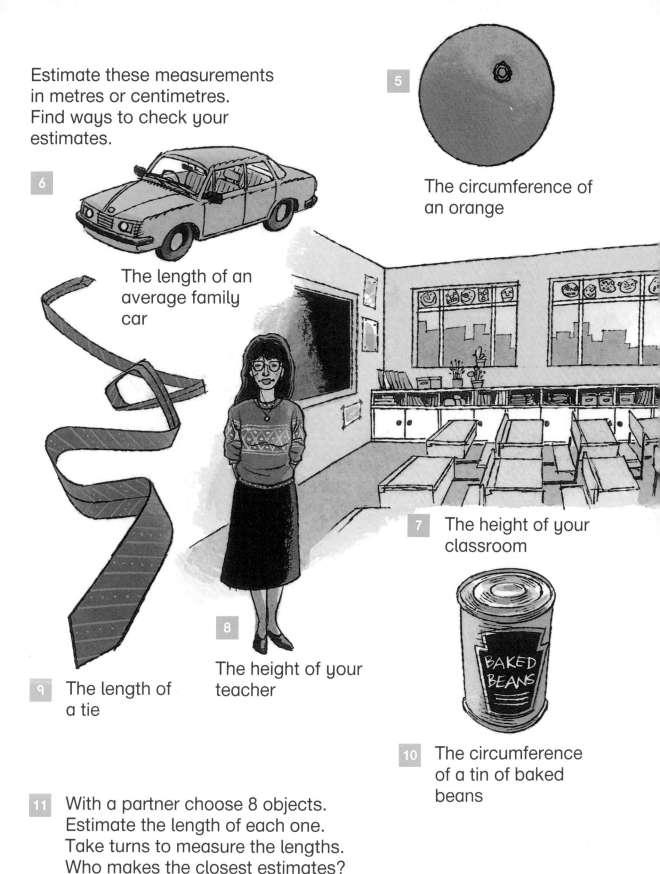

5 The circumference of
an orange

6 The length of an
average family
car

7 The height of your
classroom

8 The height of your
teacher

9 The length of
a tie

10 The circumference
of a tin of baked
beans

11 With a partner choose 8 objects.
Estimate the length of each one.
Take turns to measure the lengths.
Who makes the closest estimates?

12 Work with a friend.

Find a container that you estimate will hold about 1 litre.

Find other containers that you estimate will hold about $\frac{1}{2}$ litre, $\frac{1}{4}$ litre, 50 ml.

Now use a measuring jug and water to check how close your estimates were.

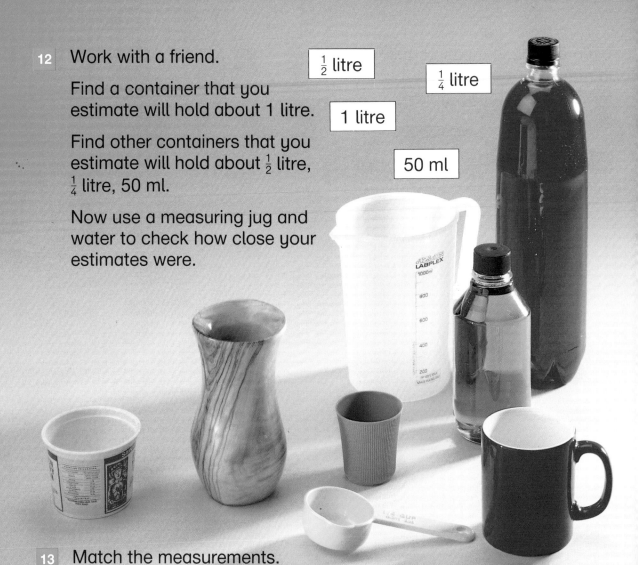

$\frac{1}{2}$ litre

$\frac{1}{4}$ litre

1 litre

50 ml

13 Match the measurements.

Write the pairs of measurements that are the same.
Which measurement is the 'odd one out'?

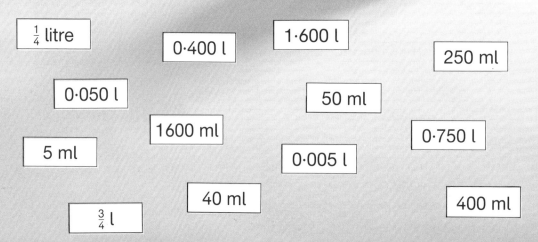

$\frac{1}{4}$ litre

0·400 l

1·600 l

250 ml

0·050 l

50 ml

1600 ml

0·750 l

5 ml

0·005 l

40 ml

400 ml

$\frac{3}{4}$ l

Work with a group of friends.

14 Weight Game.

Collect 5 objects and weigh each one.

Make a label for each weight.

Ask another group to try to match
the labels to the objects.
They can hold the objects
but they cannot weigh them.
They get a point for each correct match.

Your group must now try to match
another group's objects and labels.

15 You need bathroom scales.
Take turns to push down hard on the scales
with your left hand. Record the results.
Who can push the hardest?

16 Can you push as hard with your other hand?
Can you push twice as hard with both hands?

Let's investigate

Make a chart or diagram about yourself.
Show as many of your measurements as possible.
Try to make it interesting by using different
measures.

B

In Britain we weigh things
both in kilograms and in pounds.
Pounds (lb) are called imperial weights.
Kilograms and grams are metric weights.

1. 16 ounces (oz) = 1 lb
   How many ounces in $\frac{1}{2}$ lb, $\frac{1}{4}$ lb?

2. 1 oz is a little more than 25 g.
   Find two things that each weigh about 1 oz.
   Check their weights on the metric scales.

Change the imperial weights to metric ones.
Change the metric weights to imperial.

2 lb is about
the same as 1 kg.

Change these weights to grams.

| 9 | 1·2 kg | 10 | 3·4 kg | 11 | 2·8 kg |
| 12 | 4·5 kg | 13 | 3·25 kg | 14 | 2·75 kg |

Liquid is measured both in litres and in pints and gallons.

8 pints make 1 gallon.

1 gallon is approximately 4·5 litres.

Change these gallons to the approximate number of litres.

15 1 gallon   **16** 2 gallons   **17** 4 gallons

18 If a car travels 30 miles to the gallon, approximately how many litres will it use to travel 90 miles?

19 A mini's petrol tank holds approximately 5 gallons. About how many litres is this?

20 How many pints are approximately the same as 2 litres, 3 litres, 4 litres? Show how you worked it out.

1 litre is approximately $1\frac{3}{4}$ pints.

Metric lengths		Imperial lengths	
centimetres	(cm)	inches	(in)
metres	(m)	feet	(ft)
kilometres	(km)	yards	(yd)
		miles	

2·5 cm is about the same as 1 inch.

21 A ruler is 30 cm long.
Approximately how many inches is this?

22 Which is longer, 1 yard or 1 metre?

36 inches = 1 yd

23 In Britain we measure long distances in miles.
Name a country that measures them in km.

24 Copy and complete this table showing
miles and approximate kilometres.

8 km is about the same as 5 miles.

km	8	16	24			48	56	64		80				
miles	5			20	25				45			55	60	65	70

25 Show the information on a
straight line graph.
Choose a suitable scale.

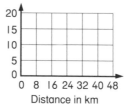

Distance in miles

Distance in km

26 Change some British speed limits to
the approximate metric ones.

27 Two French speed limits are
60 km per hour (through villages) and
90 km per hour (country roads).
Change these to approximate miles per hour.

Let's investigate

Make a list of things that are measured in imperial
measurements and some that are measured
in metric ones. Choose a variety of measures.

C

Temperature is most often measured in degrees Celsius or °C.

It is still measured in degrees Fahrenheit or °F in many places.

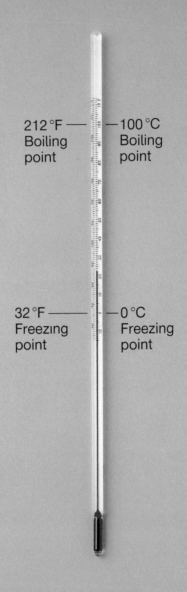

212 °F —— —100 °C
Boiling   Boiling
point   point

32 °F —— —0 °C
Freezing   Freezing
point   point

1   Use the information on the thermometer to draw a graph showing the Fahrenheit and Celsius scales.
    Join the freezing and boiling points to make a straight line graph.

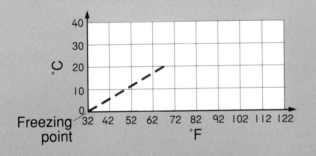

Use the graph to change these °C temperatures to the approximate °F.

2   5°C   3   20°C   4   50°C   5   80°C   6   95°C

7   Change some °F temperatures to the approximate °C.

8   What is your normal body temperature in both °C and °F?

Let's investigate

Find average miles per gallon for different makes of car.
Change the imperial measurements to the equivalent metric ones.

Number 8

1 Do these in your head.

$$\frac{48}{6} \quad \frac{24}{4} \quad \frac{30}{5} \quad \frac{36}{9}$$

$$\frac{42}{7} \quad \frac{64}{8}$$

2 Find a quick way to work these out.

$$\frac{100}{10} \quad \frac{400}{10} \quad \frac{700}{10} \quad \frac{1000}{10}$$

3 Work out each division in two different ways.

$$56 \div 4 \quad 78 \div 6$$
$$48 \div 3 \quad 70 \div 5$$

Show how you did them.

4 Find a way to do these divisions. Show your working out.

Divide 839 by 3
Divide 664 by 5
$846 \div 7$
$767 \div 6$
$$\frac{527}{4}$$

5 Find the missing numbers.

$$\square \div 6 = 32$$
$$\square \div 5 = 24$$
$$63 \div \square = 9$$
$$72 \div \square = 8$$

6 A man has 625 apples. He divides them equally into 5 boxes. How many are in each box?

7 There are 124 nuts in one jar, 116 in another and 141 in a third. What is the average number of nuts in a jar?

8 The numbers on the wheel have been mixed up.
Re-arrange them to make division sentences.

$$\square \div \square = \square$$

The answers are on the inside circle.

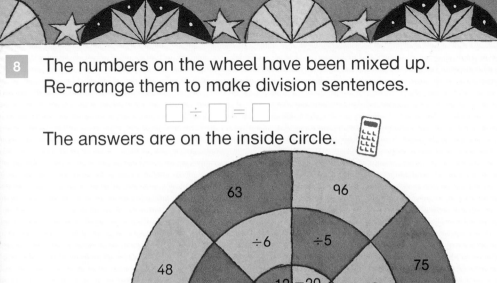

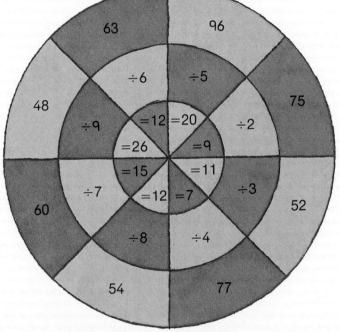

---

9 **The dice game**
Play with a friend.

Throw three dice in turn.
Use the scores to make a number.

     135

If the number will divide exactly by 3, score a point.
If the number will divide exactly by 5, score a point.
If the number will divide exactly by 3 and 5, score 2 points.
The winner is the first player to score 10 points.

Find the missing numbers.

10 1 0 2
9)⟌☐☐☐

11 1 2 2
8)⟌☐☐☐

12
  2 4 ☐
×   4
  9 7 ☐

13
  ☐ 7 6
×   2
  7 ☐ 2

Let's investigate

Find 3-digit numbers that will divide exactly by 7.
Find 3-digit numbers that have a remainder
of 3 when divided by 8.
Explain how you found them.

B

Find the missing numbers

1 ☐ ÷ 19 = 2 r 3

2 ☐ ÷ 18 = 5 r 5

3 ☐ ÷ 17 = 5 r 4

4 ☐ ÷ 24 = 4 r 3

Estimate first then give the exact answer

5 38 ÷ 19

6 87 ÷ 29

7 36 ÷ 18

8 88 ÷ 22

9 85 ÷ 17

Do these in your head

10 600 ÷ 10

11 600 ÷ 20

12 600 ÷ 30

13 800 ÷ 10

14 800 ÷ 20

15 800 ÷ 40

16 Find a way to divide 219 by 18.
Show your method clearly so that a friend can follow it.
Ask a friend to use your method to divide 246 by 19.

Four children each divided 317 by 24.
Each found a different method of doing it.
Look carefully at their methods to see how they worked it out.

Sue

$317 \div 24$

$$
\begin{array}{r}
317 \\
-24 \\
\hline
293 \\
-24 \\
\hline
269 \\
-24 \\
\hline
245 \\
-24 \\
\hline
221 \\
-24 \\
\hline
197 \\
-24 \\
\hline
173 \\
-24 \\
\hline
149 \\
-24 \\
\hline
125 \\
-24 \\
\hline
101 \\
-24 \\
\hline
77 \\
-24 \\
\hline
53 \\
-24 \\
\hline
29 \\
-24 \\
\hline
5
\end{array}
$$

13 r 5

Sasha

$317 \div 24$

1	24
2	48
4	96
8	192
16	384

$$
\begin{array}{r}
317 \\
-192 \\
\hline
125 \\
-96 \\
\hline
29 \\
-24 \\
\hline
5
\end{array}
$$

8×24

4×24

1×24

13 r. 5

Kiran

$$
\begin{array}{r}
3 \\
10 \\
24\overline{)3\,1\,7} \\
2\,40 \\
\hline
7\,7 \\
7\,2 \\
\hline
5 \quad 13\,r\,5
\end{array}
$$

Tim

$317 \div 24$

$$
\begin{array}{r}
317 \\
-240 \\
\hline
77 \\
-72 \\
\hline
5
\end{array}
$$

10×24

3×24

13 r 5

Choose one of the methods to do these.

17 $318 \div 24$ **18** $263 \div 19$

19 $336 \div 27$ **20** $351 \div 17$

21 $397 \div 18$ **22** $699 \div 17$

23 $729 \div 36$ **24** $582 \div 29$

Play a game with three friends.
Make four cards, one for each method.

Shuffle the cards and deal them out.
Work out these divisions using the method of the name on the card.
Change cards after each division.

25 $341 \div 26$ **26** $444 \div 39$

27 $308 \div 23$ **28** $331 \div 18$

29 Copy and complete the cross-number puzzle.

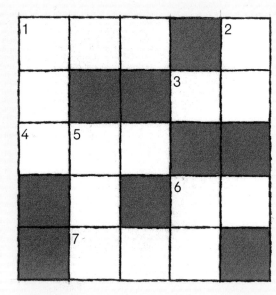

Across
1. $\square \div 26 = 16 \text{ r } 7$
3. $625 \div \square = 25$
4. $\square \div 38 = 19 \text{ r } 3$
6. $981 \div 17 = 57 \text{ r } \square$
7. $63 \times 13 = \square$

Down
1. $\square \div 17 = 23 \text{ r } 16$
2. $378 \div 15 = \square \text{ r } 3$
5. $\square \div 12 = 18 \text{ r } 2$
6. $\square \times 23 = 437$

30 Think of a number that has a remainder
of 6 if you divide it by 23, and it has
a remainder of 2 if you divide it by 24.
The number is between 50 and 100.
What is it?

Let's investigate

Write a division problem like question `30` for a friend to work out.
Try to make sure that there is only one answer.

C Five a side – a game for two players

You can estimate using any method.

Play the game with a friend.
One of you is Attack; one is Defence.

Attack sets five problems involving division by a 2 digit number.
For example ☐ ÷ 24 = 17
Defence estimates each answer as accurately as possible.
Attack checks the answer on a calculator and scores the
difference between the accurate answer and the estimated one.

Problem	Estimated answer	Calculator answer	Score
☐ ÷ 24 = 17	400 ÷ 20 = 20	408 ÷ 24 = 17	408–400 = 8
☐ ÷ 23 = 29	600 ÷ 20 = 30	667 ÷ 23 = 29	667–600 = 67

Attack totals the 5 scores.

The players then change over and play again.

The winner is the player with the highest total score.

The game can also be played by setting
multiplication problems, for example 32 × 25 = ☐

Let's investigate

The result of dividing a 3 digit number
by a 2 digit number was 50.
What might the numbers have been?
Make a chart to show possible answers.

A Using triangles

1 Draw round an equilateral triangle.
Show its axes or lines of symmetry.
How many has it got?

2 What is its order of rotational symmetry?

3 Make a chart. Record your findings.

Shape	Number of lines of symmetry	Order of rotational symmetry

Draw round equilateral triangles to make these shapes. Enter each one on the chart.

4 **5**

6 **7**

8

9 What shape have you just made?

Making patterns

10 Draw round a regular hexagon.

11 Add 6 squares to the hexagon.

12 How many lines of symmetry does the new shape have?

13 What is its order of rotational symmetry?

14 Add 3 equilateral triangles to the shape so that it now has 3 lines of symmetry and an order of rotational symmetry of 3.

15 Change the position of the 3 triangles so that the shape has a different number of lines of symmetry.

16 What is its order of rotational symmetry now?

17 Draw round an octagon. Add different shapes to change its symmetry. Record these changes.

Investigating quadrilaterals

18 Use dotty or squared paper.

Draw as many different quadrilaterals as you can.

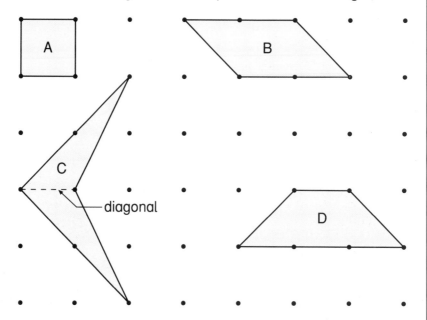

Label each one with a letter

19 Copy and complete this chart for
your quadrilaterals.

Shape	Has a diagonal that is a line of symmetry	Order of rotational symmetry
A	Yes	4

3-D shapes

A plane of symmetry splits a 3-D shape so that one half reflects the other.

You need to look at some everyday objects from home or in the classroom.

20 Work with a friend.
Discuss how many planes of symmetry each object has.

21 Find a way to record your findings.

22 Use plasticine, cubes or junk material.
Make a model that has one plane of symmetry.

Let's investigate

Draw 2-D shapes that have rotational symmetry but no line symmetry.

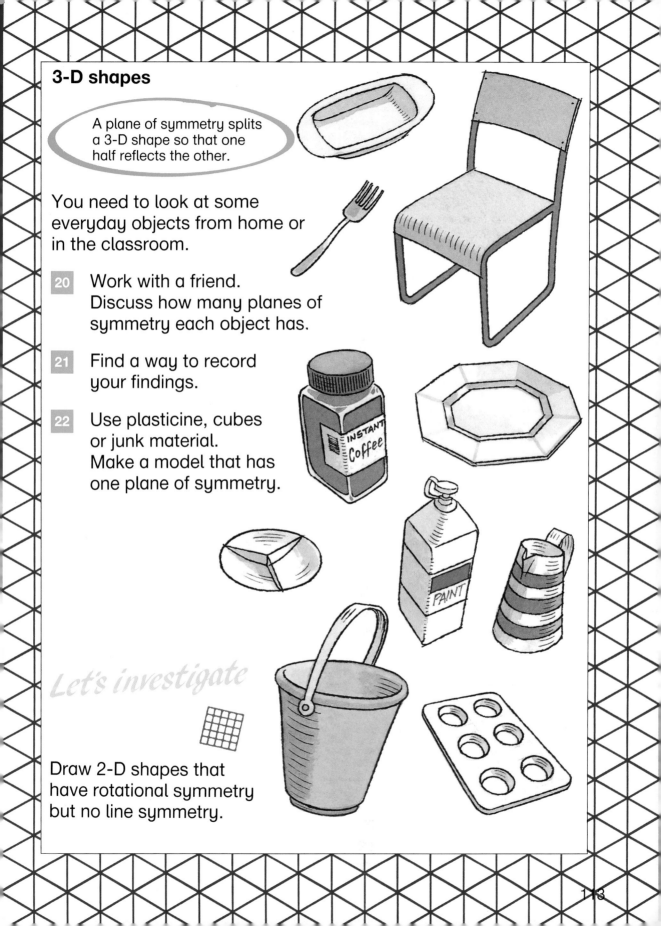

B

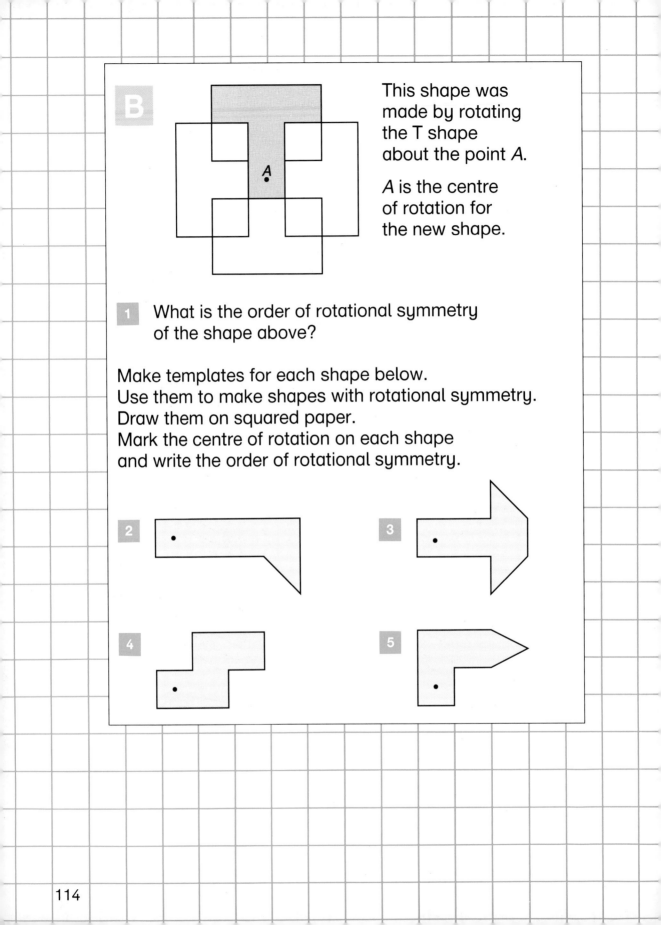

This shape was made by rotating the T shape about the point *A*.

A is the centre of rotation for the new shape.

1 What is the order of rotational symmetry of the shape above?

Make templates for each shape below.
Use them to make shapes with rotational symmetry.
Draw them on squared paper.
Mark the centre of rotation on each shape
and write the order of rotational symmetry.

2

3

4

5

114

Look at the triangular prism.

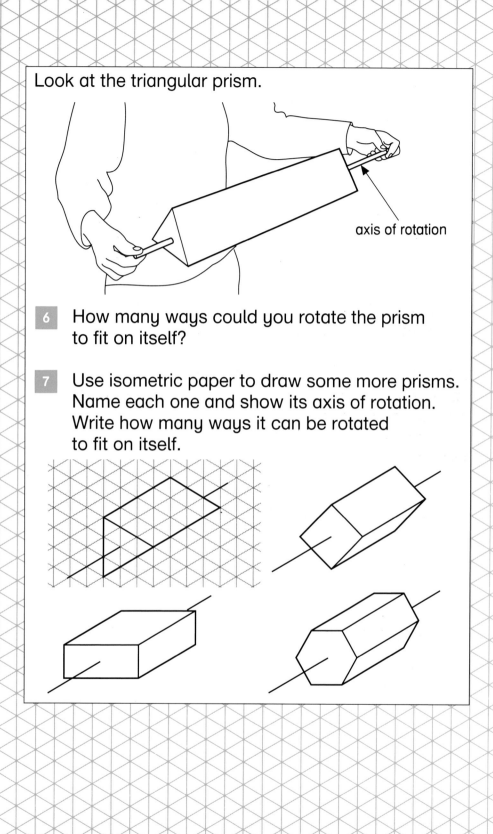

axis of rotation

6 How many ways could you rotate the prism to fit on itself?

7 Use isometric paper to draw some more prisms. Name each one and show its axis of rotation. Write how many ways it can be rotated to fit on itself.

Use boxes like these that are prisms.

Investigate each one to find out how many planes of symmetry it has.

Record your findings.

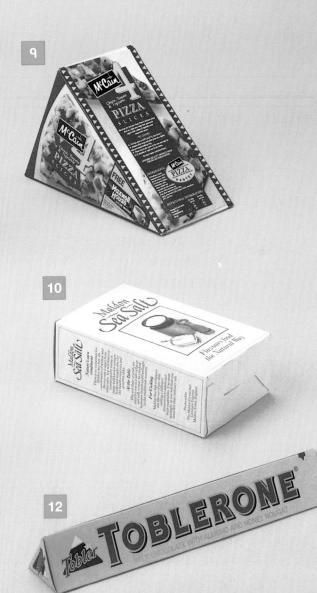

Let's investigate

Design boxes that have 1 plane of symmetry, 2 planes, 3 planes, etc.

C You need a mirror.

1. Copy the name MAY onto a piece of paper.

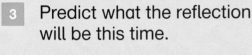

2. Predict what its reflection
will be if the mirror is
placed in this position.

    Check your prediction.

3. Predict what the reflection
will be this time.

    Check your prediction.

4. Do the same for other words putting
the mirror in both positions.

5. Can you find any words that look the same as
their reflection in one of the mirror positions?

6. Investigate numbers in this way.

Let's investigate

Can you find any letters
or numbers that look the
same as their reflection
in both mirror positions?

Can you find a word that
has horizontal and
vertical lines of
symmetry?

Number 9

1	2	3	4	5	6	7	8	9	10
11	12								20
21									30
									40
91									100

A

1 Use squared paper.

Copy and complete the 100 square.

The corner numbers in this rectangle from the 100 square add up to 29.

3	4	5	6
13	14	15	16
23	24	25	26

$3 + 26 = 29$
$23 + 6 = 29$

Use your 100 square.

2 Find other rectangles with opposite corner numbers that add up to 29.

3 Find rectangles with opposite corner numbers that add up to 32.

Choose the correct word for the following.

odd or even

4 The answer when adding two numbers next to each other horizontally on the 100 square is _____ .

5 The answer when adding two numbers next to each other vertically is _____ .

Copy and finish the following patterns

6
$1 + 2 = 3$
$3 + 4 = \square$
$5 + 6 = \square$
$7 + \square = \square$
$\square + \square = \square$

7
$1 + 2 + 3 = 6$
$3 + 4 + 5 = \square$
$5 + 6 + 7 = \square$
$7 + \square + \square = 24$
$\square + \square + \square = \square$

8
$1 + 2 + 3 + 4 = 10$
$2 + 3 + 4 + 5 = \square$
$3 + 4 + 5 + 6 = \square$
$4 + \square + \square + \square = \square$
$\square + \square + \square + \square = \square$

These animals are parts of the 100 square.
Copy them and fill in the missing numbers.
Do not look at the 100 square.

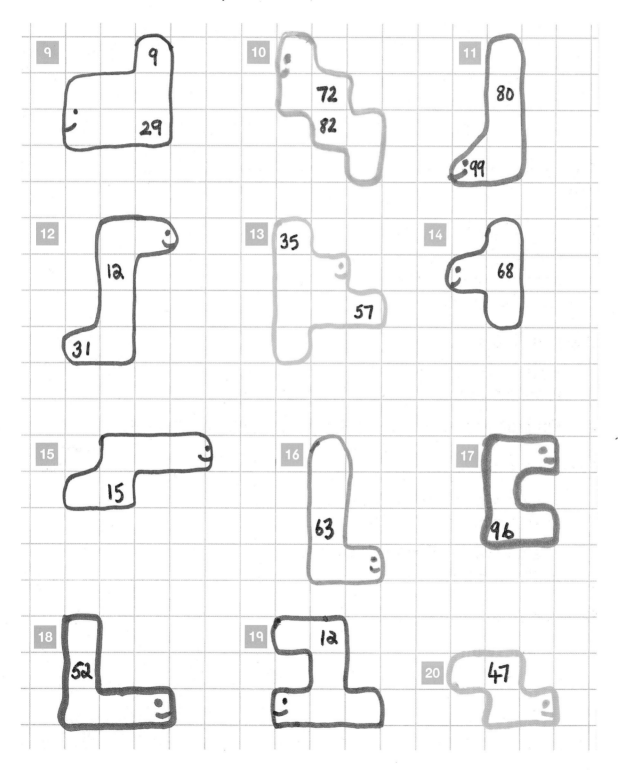

9

9

29

10

72

82

11

80

99

12

12

31

13

35

57

14

68

15

15

16

63

17

96

18

52

19

12

20

47

Copy and finish these wall patterns

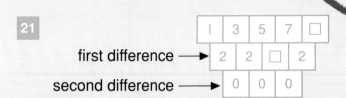

The difference between 1 and 3 is 2.

The difference between 2 and 2 is 0.

21

| 1 | 3 | 5 | 7 | ☐ |

first difference ➙ | 2 | 2 | ☐ | 2 |

second difference ➙ | 0 | 0 | 0 |

22

5	10	15	20	☐
5	5	☐	☐
0	☐	☐

23

95	88	81	☐	67
☐	☐	☐	☐
☐	☐	☐

24

4	2	☐	☐	⁻4
☐	☐	2	2
0	0	☐

25

⁻4	☐	8	14	20
☐	☐	☐	☐
☐	☐	☐

Copy and finish these number patterns.
Explain how they are made.

26 | 1 | 2 | 3 | 5 | ☐ |

27 | 2 | 5 | ☐ | 12 | 19 |

28 | 13 | 8 | 5 | ☐ | 2 |

29 | 16 | 10 | 6 | ☐ | 2 |

Let's investigate

Find a way to complete
the number pattern.

| ☐ | ☐ | ☐ | ☐ | 11 |

Find three other ways
to do it.

B Square numbers

These are found by counting the number of small squares in the pattern.

1   4   9   16

---

1   Copy and complete the pattern of square numbers.

1	4	9	16	☐	☐	☐
1×1	2×2	3×3	4×4	☐ × ☐	☐ × ☐	☐ × ☐
1^2	2^2	3^2	4^2	☐^{2}	☐^{2}	☐^{2}

2   Copy and finish the following pattern.

$1 = 1^2$

$1 + 3 = 2^2$

$1 + 3 + 5 = ☐^2$

$1 + 3 + 5 + 7 = ☐^2$

$☐ + ☐ + ☐ + ☐ + ☐ = ☐^2$

3^2 means 3×3 or 3 squared.

3   Explain what is happening to the numbers and the dot pattern.

Find these triples.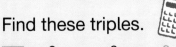

4 $3^2 + 4^2 = ☐^2$

5 $6^2 + ☐^2 = 10^2$

6 $☐^2 + 12^2 = 15^2$

7 $☐^2 + 12^2 = 13^2$

The numbers found by counting the number of dots inside each triangle are called triangle numbers.

1   3   6   10   15

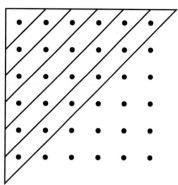

8 Continue the pattern of triangular numbers.

1   3   6   10   15   ☐   ☐

9 Continue the pattern of square numbers made by adding two triangular numbers until you get to 36.

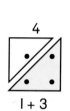 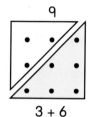 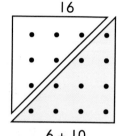

4   9   16

1 + 3   3 + 6   6 + 10

Cube numbers

2^3 means $2 \times 2 \times 2$ or 2 cubed.

1	8	27	64
$1 \times 1 \times 1$	$2 \times 2 \times 2$	$3 \times 3 \times 3$	$4 \times 4 \times 4$
1^3	2^3	3^3	4^3

10 Which is the next cube number after 64?

11 Which number cubed is 343?

12 Copy this pattern and find the missing numbers.

$$1 = 1 = 1^3$$
$$3 + 5 = 8 = 2^3$$
$$7 + 9 + 11 = \square = \square^3$$
$$\square + \square + \square + \square = \square = \square^3$$

13 Which two numbers in the pattern are both square and cube?

Put the numbers 1 to 10 into these machines.
Write the patterns.

14 INPUT → ☐ × 2 → OUTPUT
multiple of 2

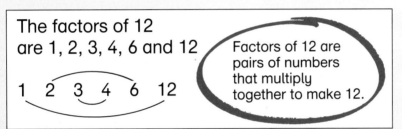

Multiples of 2
are found by
multiplying 2 by
whole numbers.
2, 4, 6, 8, 10, . . .

15 INPUT → ☐ × 3 → OUTPUT
multiple of 3

Find which numbers the following sets are multiples of.

16 25, 30, 55   **17** 20, 70, 90   **18** 14, 28, 70

19 Find three numbers that are multiples of 3 and 4.

20 Find three numbers that are multiples of 2 and 5.

The factors of 12
are 1, 2, 3, 4, 6 and 12

1 2 3 4 6 12

Factors of 12 are
pairs of numbers
that multiply
together to make 12.

Write all the pairs of factors of the
following numbers.

21 16   **22** 20

23 36   **24** 30

This is a factor plant for 18.

25 Draw factor plants
for 24 and 42.

Eratosthenes' method for finding prime numbers

1 has only itself as a factor and so is not a prime number. Cross it out.

2 is a prime number. It has only two factors 1 and itself. All other multiples of 2 have more than two factors so cross them out.

3 is prime. It has only two factors. Cross out the multiples of 3.

5 is the next prime number. Cross out all its multiples.

Continue this method of crossing out multiples. The numbers not crossed out are the prime numbers.

Eratosthenes was a Greek astronomer who invented a method for finding prime numbers. It is known as the sieve of Eratosthenes.

A prime number has exactly one pair of factors, 1 and the number itself.

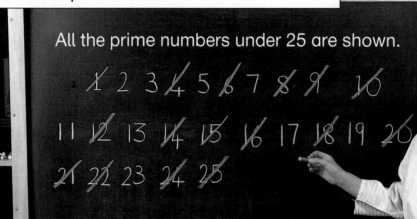

All the prime numbers under 25 are shown.

1 2 3 4 5 6 7 8 9 10
11 12 13 14 15 16 17 18 19 20
21 22 23 24 25

Prickly Or

26 Use a 100 square and Eratosthenes' method to find all the prime numbers up to 100.

27 Find the next two prime numbers after 100.

28 Find 5 pairs of prime numbers that add up to 78.

Let's investigate

Square numbers   1 4 9 16 25 36 49 64 81 100

Find some prime numbers that are the sum of two square numbers.

C

$9 = 3 \times 3$

1 Write five numbers between 1 and 50 that have a pair of factors which are both the same number.

What number when multiplied by itself gives the following?

2 81 **3** 100 **4** 16

Enter 64 on the calculator.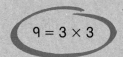

Press the square root button $\sqrt{}$. What do you notice?

5 The square root of 64 is ☐

$\sqrt{64} =$ ☐

6 Use a calculator to find the square root of each of these numbers.

289 10 000 36
144 169 484
121 5329

7 Multiply each answer by itself. Explain what you find.

8 Find 3 more numbers that have square roots that are whole numbers.

Let's investigate

Find the number

It is a multiple of 3.
It is one less than a prime number.
It is a factor of 72.
It is not a triangular number.

Make up some of your own.

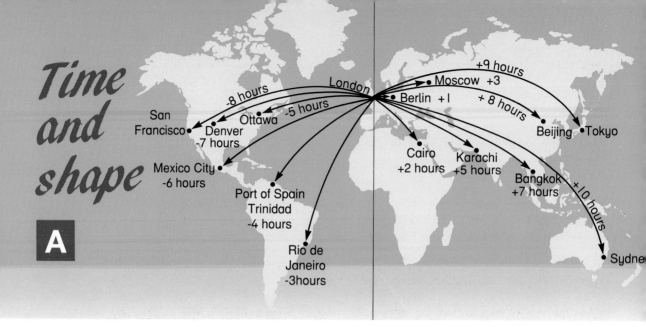

Time and shape

A

The earth rotates once every 24 hours and the
sun rises at different times around the world.
Because of this the world is divided into time zones.
The time at Greenwich, London is the standard time.
Places to the east of Greenwich are ahead of it in time (+hours).
Places to the west of it are behind it in time (−hours).

At 12:00 or midday in Britain it is 13:00 hours in Berlin.

1 Copy the charts and write the missing times.

London	Thursday	12:00
Moscow		
Cairo		
Mexico City		
San Francisco		
Tokyo		
Beijing		

London	Monday	08:00
Denver		
Rio de Janeiro		
Bangkok		
Karachi		
Ottawa		
Sydney		

Let's investigate

Choose one of the cities and plan times of phone
calls from there to people in 5 of the other cities.
Each person must receive the call at 12:00 local time.
Choose another city and do the same.

This is a network diagram
of part of a road system.
A node is where roads meet.
An arc is a road or line that joins nodes.
A region is an area separated by arcs.

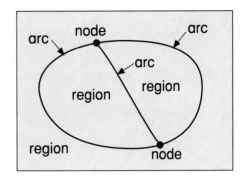

Try to draw each network diagram without taking your pencil off the paper or going over the same line twice.

Write which shapes you can do this with and which you cannot.

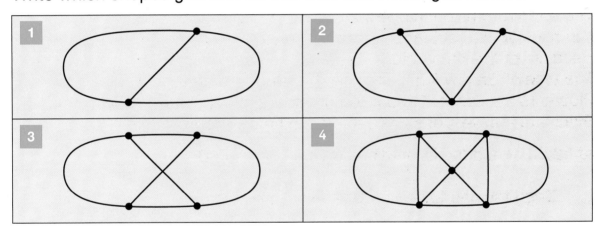

5. Count the number of nodes, regions and arcs for each network diagram.
Copy and complete the chart.

	Nodes	Regions	Arcs
1	2		

Let's investigate

Make up some more network diagrams.
Count the number of nodes, regions and arcs.
Enter the numbers in your chart.
What do you notice about the numbers for nodes, regions and arcs?

Many years ago the people of Koenigsberg in Russia
tried to find out if they could start anywhere and
cross all of their seven bridges once only, in one walk.

1 Draw a network diagram for the Koenigsberg bridges.
Can you draw the diagram, crossing each of the 7 bridges once
only, without taking your pencil off the paper?

Let's investigate

Put another bridge in the network diagram.
Find if it is possible to cross all the bridges once
only on one walk now. Explain your findings.